180 Days of Making

How to incorporate experiential learning in ways that will change the world for your students.

MICHELLE CARLSON

Foreward by Dale Dougherty

ISBN:
ISBN-10: 1535582898
ISBN-13: 978-1535582896

Shout out to the rad peeps who provided design, photography,
and made sure all the words were in the right order :-)

Cover design: Heather Vine of Vine Design
Interior illustrations: Thanks Adobe Capture app!
Editor: Jonna Hawker Turek

Dedicated to all of the kids out there who yearn for a more joyful school experience and all of the educators who work tirelessly to make it happen.

Contents

Foreward

One of the most telling comments I hear from teachers who engage their students in making is: "This is why I went into teaching in the first place!" It conveys their own excitement and conviction that what they can do as a teacher really matters not just to them personally but to their students. Michelle Carlson is one of those teachers who truly loves what she does but also what she is able to accomplish: creating positive and supportive context for the social, emotional and intellectual growth of young people.

The promise of engaging children in making is that it applies to all children, not just a few talented kids. It applies to children at any age and at every level of education. Making can be a broad framework that can include many different styles of learning and many different kinds of outcomes, many of which are not supported in traditional academic education. Making encourages the development of creative and innovative thinkers and do-ers whvo learn to trust new ideas and test them out by developing and sharing their work. We call it the "maker mindset." It can become a toolset for living an independent life, developing one's own capabilities by becoming a productive learner.

In this book, Michelle shares with all of us what she has learned from her own practical experiences working with students and setting up makerspaces. She tackles some of the challenges that any teacher would face in convincing students (and administration) that there's a better way to learn. She shares how she organized a class on a week-to-week plan that will undoubtedly make it easier for other teachers to get started. However, there is no formula, no plan, no one pattern that will work for every teacher or every student. That's the challenging part for a teacher but it is also what makes the effort rewarding. It requires not just understanding how to engage kids in making, but how to organize education around a passion for learning that includes exploration, experimentation and creative expression.

Dale Dougherty

Preface

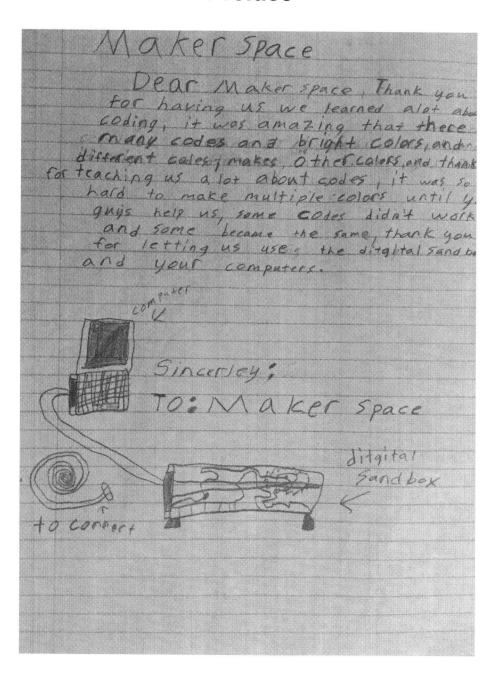

Maker Space

Dear Maker space, Thank you for having us we learned alot about coding, it was amazing that there many codes and bright colors, and different codes makes Other colors, and thank for teaching us a lot about codes, it was so hard to make multiple colors until y. guys help us, some codes didn't work and some became the same, thank you for letting us use the ditgital sandbox and your computers.

computer

Sincerley;

TO: Maker Space

ditgital Sandbox

to connect

What is making and why should you care?

> **"Making is imagining, conceptualizing, designing, building and re-building. It is creation of concept at its most fundamental level, and can be used to make things, prove or disprove ideas, or to create function, wisdom, or folly. Children learn to love the process, and lives change through making."**
> **- Rick Fitzpatrick, Superintendent**

Making is quite possibly the easiest and most cost effective way to change the world for *all* kids. It's more than just learning by doing, it is a philosophy that embraces student voice, giving kids a vehicle to personally connect with education in profound and exciting ways.

As a kid, I hated school. It was irrelevant and boring and never offered options to approach the journey in ways that made sense to me. Today, there are millions of kids who feel this way, and they are desperate for something more.

You know who else hated school? Albert Einstein, Plato, Mark Twain, Oscar Wilde, Winston Churchill, George Bernard Shaw, Thomas Edison, Henry David Thoreau, Benjamin Franklin, Theodore Roosevelt, Ralph Waldo Emerson, Robert Frost, Margaret Mead, Anne Sullivan... the list goes on and on.

Some of the most respected, creative, and brilliant minds in history have shared sentiments like this quote from Thoreau, "What does education often do? It makes a straight-cut ditch of a free, meandering brook."

We lose the attention and squash the inspiration of our most treasured resource by not recognizing the need for change, for joy, and personalization in learning. Education does not have to be awful, and being better does not have to cost billions of dollars. Making, and the Maker Movement offer a level of hope and real possibility like nothing else can, and this book provides a strong, real-world, kid and teacher tested plan to turn it all around.

On the following pages, you'll find all of the materials you need to offer a whole year of making for your students. In Rick Fitzpatricks's words (the superintendent of the district we implemented this program in), "These materials and lessons are a treasure."

We've also provided lots of background on the Maker Movement, inspiring stories of real kids and teachers and guidance from the experts who made it happen here in our community.

> *This is the documentary style story of a program that started as a dream, became a reality over one summer and in a single school year, permanently changed the lives of the students and teachers who participated in it.*

As leaders in education, we have a responsibility to the children of this nation to provide them with rich, engaging, real-world environments that build a lifelong love of learning.

We did that in the middle school elective class called "Adventures in Making." The plan came together beautifully and we feel a strong sense of social responsibility to share that plan, so you have the support you need to create these life-changing programs for your kids.

This story, is one of 180 days of triumph, with a group of amazing kids, teachers, and school leaders. Hence the name, *180 Days of Making*.

The school featured is comprised of:

60.65% Hispanic students
25.44% English Language Learners
76.92% participating in free or reduced price lunch program
(source: California Department of Education 2015-2016 school year)

It's important for you to have this data as a frame of reference; it offers a snapshot of where our kids were coming from. What it doesn't offer are their stories, or their unique humanity, which you will find sprinkled throughout the book. Data will only get us so far, and it's important to remember, always, that we are working with people, not numbers.

Adventures in Making supported the growth and development of students who know poverty, struggle with language, and often times suffer from the challenges of living in poor rural neighborhoods with access to few resources.

Despite these challenges, the program was hugely successful and was due in no small part to the dedicated team of people who supported it, helping bring this vision to life, for all kids.

Three of these people have agreed to dive in and help bring this book to the world for the benefit of growing the magic of makerspace programs and, in turn, the success of our country's greatest resource. Rick Fitzpatrick, district superintendent, Phil Mishoe, makerspace teacher and Noelle McDaniel, educational technology curriculum support provider are here as well, to share their insights, suggestions, wisdom and experiences.

Including their voices in *180 Days of Making* means you are not just getting my view and advice. You are getting the teacher's, the curriculum supporter's and the superintendent's points of view as well.

What follows is a holistic, multi-faceted playbook of sorts - from both the 20,000 foot level and the day-to-day detail. The book includes all of the tools you need to go forth and help your students conquer learning in ways that inspire, empower and encourage.

The kids who signed up for Adventures in Making signed up for a lot of different reasons. Some wanted an easy class, others thought it would be "kinda cool." Every single one of them signed up because they were looking for something different, and that's what we gave them.

What they didn't know, was that this was the class that would teach them how to love learning again.

Without realizing it, they found themselves learning and *enjoying the process*. Yep, that's right! This was the case, even when it got tough, challenging and sometimes frustrating. Instead of giving up, the kids were invigorated, because for a lot of them, this was their first experience at struggling, learning resilience and figuring out how to keep going.

What came out of this year was nothing short of amazing, and I don't say that lightly. The kids who were shy, disconnected, and unaware of their unique interests and skills became an exuberant community of learners, who found themselves, and found their way to connect with and support one another in their quest for learning that meant something to them personally. Learning that was joyful.

A lot of people scoff at the words "joyful learning." People at all different levels in the education system tell us not to use that word. That it takes the focus away from the things that purportedly prepare students for success. In the absence of joy, however, learning is nothing more than memorizing facts required for a grade or a test, and is not maintained past that point. Joyful learning is the kind of experience that stays with you for a lifetime and truly prepares young people for success in adulthood.

In interviewing and working with many a student over the years, I have found joy to be a very effective method in bringing learning to life and making it stick. Without it, all you have is a mechanical process that isn't appealing to anyone, student or teacher.

> *Outside of school, students are kids. They are people who love to laugh and play and have fun. Imagine what school could be if we were to bring the world of the "kid" and the world of the "student" together.*

It's about time we step up and give kids what they truly need to move into adulthood with skills beyond math and reading. It's time we give them the necessary skills to build the future.

> *This is what the Maker Movement offers: engagement in learning because you want to learn, not because you're being graded on it.*

My vision is for all students to have the opportunity to experience the joyful and relevant education they deserve. We can make this happen. We did make this happen with Adventures in Making and the great news is: we can do it without wasting billions of dollars on quick fixes, magic bullets and boxed solutions. We can do it by embracing the Maker Movement and by committing to it long term. Our kids deserve this and the future of our country depends on it.

The Maker Movement breathes life back into learning for all.

Thank you for purchasing this book! I hope you enjoy the journey as much as I did. My team and I are excited to welcome you to the world of Making. Read on for the lesson plans, activities, videos and re-sources we created to support you in your journey. Take this torch and run with it.

Go for a grand slam and turn your classroom or school into a place of self discovery and learning that is exciting and joyful - for you and your kids. And most importantly, turn it into a place where every single young person can find their passion and learn how to pursue their dreams.

Our "Why"

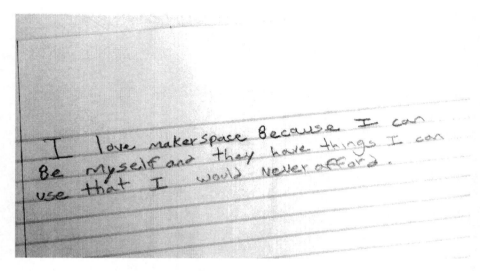

The written statement above says it all. This came from one of our kids when we asked them to give us some feedback on what Adventures in Making meant to them.

The goal of this work is to support you in becoming a Maker Educator, which will transform learning in your classroom, school or district. Making has the power to activate the following for every child: passion for learning, intrinsic motivation to understand, and the ability to define success on a personal level. As Rick says, "Huge change *does* happen."

We work with kids from all backgrounds - from the straight A students to the ones who face unimaginable struggles and challenges every day - and we love them all. Because of our location in a rural community plagued by generational poverty, gang and drug issues and high unemployment, we work mostly with kids who would fit the label of being "at risk."

Making resonates with all of them. Every single one. From those who redefine the label of "at risk" like Maryn, who you will meet here in a few minutes, to the ones we work with who are incarcerated and on a trajectory that is just as terrifying for them as it is for the community in which they live.

They are all equally touched and equally invigorated by having opportunities to be heard, to be themselves, heck, *to create themselves*...and to connect all of those things to something real. Better yet, Making cultivates skills that ensure all kids are equally equipped to do something wonderfully fulfilling and positive with their lives. It's not just fun and games or play time, Making is the thing that will create bona fide futures for *all* of our kids.

That is our *why*. And it's why we will work tirelessly to bring this magic to as many kids as we possibly can with the resources we have.

In 2011, author and famous TED Talk presenter Simon Sinek published a book titled *Start With Why: How Great Leaders Inspire Everyone To Take Action*. If you haven't watched the TED Talk, or read the book, we highly recommend both of them. Sinek has a knack for explaining the concept of starting with why and the powerful impact it allows you to have on the world around you.

Our why is simple: we want school to be a joyful place where kids are given every opportunity to develop useful skills, their understanding of the world around them and how they fit into it. We want them to have experiences which help them grow and become young adults who are capable and successful contributors to a better tomorrow.

We know that Making is the pathway to such an outcome.

But don't take our word for it. This book is filled with the stories and testimonials of the young people we've worked with. Stories of their desperate need for education to be the things we've described above, and stories of how Making filled that empty space with something that changed, and even saved, lives.

To get us started, here is one of those stories:

> Hello my name is Maryn and I am a Makerspace success story, but not a typical one. I was the child no one thought needed saving until it was clear I needed saving. I was valedictorian of my graduating class this last year. Now I don't say that to be prideful, I only say that to give you perspective about me. After knowing that, what comes to mind when you think of me? Admiration towards my accomplishments, positivity because I am a child flourishing in the system? That I'm a Success?
>
> Now there is a kid sitting in the back of the classroom. Disengaged, serious, with zero drive, failing every class. What comes to mind when you think of him? Frustration because you want him to be better? Sadness because if only he applied himself, he could do well? He is failing his classes, do you see him as a failure?
>
> You're not alone, we all do it. Labels are an easy, convenient, and extremely dangerous game to play.
>
> What if I told you that every day when I came home from school, after sports practice, after community service, I would sit down to do my homework and just bawl. The expectation of success, whether people admit putting it on me or not, transformed into a

deep-seated fear of failure. That was too much to bear and I became depressed. Not sad, depressed with sporadic suicidal thoughts.

During my time in the makerspace, I've seen kids labeled as "failures" creating graphic designs and animations for promo videos that were so professional looking that I actually made them prove to me that they hadn't just pulled them off the internet - creating it all from scratch with no expert telling them what to do, no traditional class, nothing except their personal drive to learn how to do it, because they wanted to learn.

Isn't that what education is about? A child with such a burning desire to learn something that when given the raw materials and resources, they use their love to pursue the knowledge themselves.

As for me, I honestly thought that makerspace would look great on a college application. It seemed fun but mostly the name "Makerspace Ambassador" would be so unique to the college boards. In the makerspace I learned the importance of failing, and the even greater importance of not being bogged down by failure and getting back up and trying again and again. I thought I knew how to do this before, but I didn't.

With no expectations of success I felt free to experiment and truly learn.

So you see the makerspace is a place for every child. The perfect student, the slacker, the social butterfly, or the outcast. In the makerspace there are no expectations, no labels, we bring together kids from all different social backgrounds and back stories to come together and share their love and passion for learning and exploring. In fact one of my closest friends I only met through the makerspace. We were in different circles but being together and working on projects together at the makerspace gave us a good working, mutually respecting partnership and friendship.

In two sentences the makerspace teaches you the stuff you don't learn in the classroom, by applying all of the classroom stuff. And, for most of us it teaches us how to love learning again.

Maryn presented her story in person at a regional County Superintendent's Symposium in the summer of 2015. She spoke very passionately about her experiences in school, the struggles she faced as the "perfect" kid, and how the makerspace saved her.

Before that presentation where she bared her soul, no one was aware Maryn was struggling like this. No one knew the pain she was suffering inside. She hid it well. On the outside, she was happy, pleasant to be around, put together. Definitely not identified as "at risk."

There are a lot of Maryns out there who need us, but can't allow themselves to be vulnerable enough to reach out and say it.

She is now off to college, majoring in mathematics and doing fabulously well, thanks to the life skills and strong sense of self she developed during her time in the makerspace.

We all know kids who need that extra *something* in order to reach their full potential, and many times, no matter how many services we bring to them, it's simply not enough. Because ultimately, it must come from within.

Programs such as the one detailed in 180 Days of Making offer a real solution, for the straight A student, the failing student, and all ranges of students in between. They accomplish this by building power within each student to be resilient, make choices, persevere, and to truly see their future as something they have the power to create. That they are not just participants in a world run by others; they are the ones who have the capacity to create the world they want to live in. To build their own version of the American Dream.

Making is at the root of the American Dream, which according to Wikipedia "implies an opportunity for Americans to achieve prosperity through hard work. According to The Dream, this includes the opportunity for one's children to grow up and receive a good education and career without artificial barriers. It is the opportunity to make individual choices without the prior restrictions that limited people according to their class, caste, religion, race, or ethnicity."

The Dream proclaims that "all men are created equal" with the right to "Life, Liberty and the pursuit of Happiness."

That's what we want right? Prosperity? A willingness of citizens to work hard to achieve goals, and a common agreement that we all have the right to pursue happiness?

We have an opportunity in our schools to lay the groundwork for life, liberty and the pursuit of happiness. Those characteristics come easily for programs steeped in the Maker philosophy.

Making offers young people opportunities to explore many topics, identify the ones that speak to them and dive deeply into those topics, with the tools, support, and encouragement necessary to pursue interests beyond what is required for a grade or a test.

> *Making is learning how to create a space in your mind that houses your imagination and your self-image. It allows you to create your own story of what you can be and do.*

For kids like Maryn, and the others whose lives were touched profoundly, these programs are what made the difference. The difference between a challenging life lacking in true joy and the ability to see the importance of joy and creativity in one's pursuit of academic and professional success.

School must be a place where young people get to explore, be curious, cultivate and hone emotional intelligence, allowing them to define themselves in the context of their community and the world.

The answer is Maker education and right now, the Maker Movement is taking education by storm. An exciting shift is beginning to happen and students are starting to connect with learning in ways that inspire not only them, but also their teachers and their school leaders, who are seeing the possibility and potential of what *can be* once again.

Together we will support one another in bringing the vision of what *can be* to life - and keeping that vision alive - in our schools, because our ultimate goal is to prepare kids for their future. In order to prepare kids for successful - and joyful - futures, we need more programs such as this one.

This book offers you a way to get started. It builds on the "why" and includes the "how" - from summer planning through the last day of school. It provides the day to day structure of activities with clear and easy to follow steps to make it happen.

Moreover, it includes advice and perspectives from a diverse set of education leaders. In the following chapters, we take all of what we know from these people, as well as our own human intuition about the way things work, and apply it; giving you a tried and true road map to success.

This book isn't intended to tell you the only way it can happen or give you a lock-step, turnkey solution. It's intended to give you everything we did to make it happen in our schools, so you have a starting point for bringing this kind of amazing learning and change to yours.

> *There are kids like Maryn all over the world who are depending on us.*

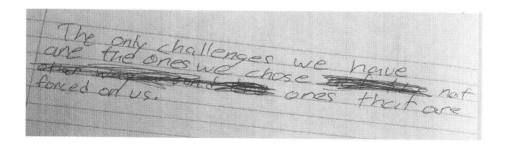

The Recipe for Success

Everyone likes a recipe, so here it is, in elegant simplicity:

You can just about guarantee success in a makerspace program when you have the following three things solidly in place:

Leadership support
Proper equipment and supplies
The right people leading the class

Seems like a no brainer, right? After several years doing this work, We've come across far too many passionate and dedicated educators with stories of rock solid starts and disappointing ends in creating these programs. So, as much of a no brainer as these three things seem to be, it's clear we need more support in bringing them into focus.

A huge part of our "why" for writing this book is to offer support and a clear path to success for every person seeking to bring joyful and relevant learning to schools across our nation and beyond. It is our sincere hope that, in providing this information, you'll have more of what you need to develop your vision for your Maker program, and to surmount any challenges you find along the way.

The goal isn't just to start something great. It's just as important - and challenging - to create something that can withstand the test of time in our schools.

Knowing the recipe up front, and insisting that these three things are taken care of before you dive head first into creating a makerspace at your school will save you a great deal of heartache (and headaches) in the long run. It will also help to ensure that your efforts are generative. This is the kind of work that has the potential to change lives like nothing else. We've seen firsthand how makerspaces create a lasting, positive impact for individual children and entire communities when implemented with fidelity to the Maker philosophy.

Take Ericka, for example. One day, during her senior year, she said to me, "I have always thought I was stupid. I've never really been good at school and I've never done well on tests. Passing is how kids are measured and graded and if we can't pass the tests, we must not be good at anything."

What she said next filled me with an overwhelming sense of hope:

> *"That's what I've always thought…until I met you. You saw something in me that I didn't even know was there. You told me I was good at something. You gave me a way to believe in myself and to know that even if I'm not good at passing tests, that doesn't mean I'm not smart. Now I know I am smart and that I can DO THINGS. Now I know that I can have the future that I want for myself."*

With so much potential for greatness, you want your time and investment to really count when you dive into a project like this.

Here we go! Let's unpack the three integral pieces, shall we?

Leadership Support:

First and foremost, you need support from someone who has the power and authority to remove road blocks, make tough, important decisions and help you find funding, is one of the most critical pieces for you as a Maker Movement trailblazer. Because in the long run, you can have a rock star teacher and all the stuff in the world to work with, but if your leadership isn't on board, you may find yourself standing alone with no one to champion the work or help to move it forward. We don't want to belabor this point as every person reading this right now can recall a scenario when leadership was key to making something happen. We all know how leadership can make or break just about everything in our education system.

Luckily, for those of us bringing the Adventures in Making elective class to life in Corning, we had district superintendent, Rick Fitz-patrick. Rick identified the Maker elective as a priority and offered fantastic support across the board to those of us who were tasked with getting it up and running.

Because of his support and leadership, the program took off and soared to heights that amazed us all. Rick's collaboration on the project is a huge piece of why it was so successful. Rick taught us that people need a recipe. After lots of experiences, challenges, and successes, we have created an easy to follow recipe for a wildly successful Maker program. You can be confident that if you follow it to a tee and stick to it, it will not fail.

> *To sum it up, leadership support means consistent, long-term support of the vision, unblocking the road and figuring out the money.*

Proper Equipment and Supplies:

Unlike the leadership piece, which is pretty defined, the supplies piece is much more flexible in what it can look like.

You can have a makerspace that looks like a shop class, or you can have one that focuses on art, sewing, or high end technology. I have found, at least for middle school, it's great to have a broad range, including art and relatively inexpensive supplies like craft sticks, duct tape and paper clips, alongside technology like iMacs and robotics equipment.

We are especially inspired by the things students create when they have high tech as well as no tech options to work with in an environment that affords them the freedom to explore these diverse materials on their own terms.

It is also important to point out not all highly successful and engaging makerspaces have a 3D printer. Ours didn't. Our experience with these devices has been that they are sometimes pesky, most times expensive, and always slow to produce a print.

3D printers are amazing and absolutely have a place in the world of fabrication and design, but if you're on a budget, look for less expensive tools and definitely don't discount the importance of art and creativity in your Maker program. These things allow students to fluidly and organically explore the wonderful connections between science, technology, engineering and math.

We expect that the time will come when 3D printers are able to produce items faster and are less expensive to own. When that day arrives, we will enthusiastically explore them as a necessary tool in a Maker classroom.

From a high level overview perspective, we like to focus on stocking makerspaces with supplies and equipment which allow students to imagine, build, iterate, and ultimately develop skills such as perseverance, decision making, communication, and problem solving. Honing these skills will help tremendously as young learners travel through the stages of their life, and can be applied to any career path they choose to pursue.

> *The most important tool in the room is the individual and collective minds of the students. Everything we do must be in support of activating those tools.*

For a deeper dive into the various types of makerspaces, equipment lists and so on, you can check out the resources our friends at the Maker Education Initiative (makered.org) offer in their various Makerspace Playbooks. And we will, of course, share the list of things we purchased for the Corning program later on in this book.

The right people leading the class:

Finally, and equally important, is having the right person or people leading your program or class. You will likely have a "teacher" who is responsible for the day to day activities, but you are looking for that teacher who sees him/herself as a coach and mentor; not the person who is most comfortable standing up front *teaching the class*.

Maker programs are very different from your traditional classroom, as they are almost entirely student driven. Again, there are a lot of variables here and we've seen these programs take on many different forms, but in order for it to truly honor the Maker philosophy, a focus on student choice and student voice is paramount.

The right person understands how to lead in ways that empower students to lead also, and each student's experience in the program will be unique to them.

> ***Your "right person" is the one who is comfortable stepping back, and allowing the students to step up.***

It's the person who doesn't feel the need to control every aspect of the classroom, and instead is happy to allow the students the freedom to explore, fail, struggle, and learn from their experiences. In this particular story, that person was Phil Mishoe - and before the makerspace - he was the school's P.E. teacher.

Phil did a podcast, which you can find on our website (www.future-developmentgroup.com), and also transcribed in the back of the book. It's a great introduction to what this all looks like from the teacher's perspective. Phil's tremendous success leading the class reminded us it's not the title, or the degree, or the type of credential you look for when searching for that "right person." It's the person who is open, positive and willing to work with you, who will make magic happen for your kids.

So, there it is. The recipe. If, after reading this, you are unsure about any of these three pieces, focus your efforts here; get the recipe for success happily bubbling away and then move forward with a sense of joy, knowing that you're choosing to focus your energy and efforts in ways that will allow you to move forward and bring the magic of Making to life in your school.

By focusing your efforts in ways that allow you to create maximum impact, you can also take great pride in the fact you are paving the way so your community's children can have bright futures - in jobs they love. Because of that, you are doing a great service for the future of this country, as well.

> ***Build your program out from a strong, focused foundation that is do-able and use that to leverage sustainability and growth.***

Open-Ended Exploration & Creative Play

Full access to all tools, resources & supplies

Instant immersion into Maker environment, but with no initial expectation to produce

Guided Projects With 2-3 Choices

Full access to all of the tools, resources and supplies of the Makerspace

As we progress along this continuum, students become better able to think critically, assess situations and make decisions

Open-Ended Short-Term Project With Virtually Endless Choices

The world is your oyster... students decide, plan, pitch, execute plan, present your work

Feedback loop is especially critical at this point as students have ventured into new territory and will need positive reinforcement to foster intrinsic motivation

Continuing to add depth and complexity. Also continuing to provide increase in choices. *Feedback loop continues to be critical*

Beginning to see the following:
1. Increased desire to have choice & freedom and a higher comfort level with those things
2. Ability to take on more challenging projects
3. Ability to reflect on process and to think ahead/set goals

Difficulty with having and making choices → Ability to make good choices and an understanding of how to learn independently

Quiet students, not comfortable discussing or collaborating → Students easily discuss topics, work through challenges, support one another

Short, simple projects → Longer, more complex projects

FEEDBACK LOOP:
Trying something new
Taking a risk

Internal sense of accomplishment
(I think I did a good job!)

External positive feedback
(You think I did a good job!)

DAY 1 ← ← ←

DAY 180 ← ← ←

STUDENTS SKILLS & ABILITIES INCREASE

Intrinsically motivated to learn

Self efficacy

Understanding of how things work

Increased ability to work collaboratively (and ENJOY it!) and participate in group projects.

Increased ability to persevere and create solutions to challenges/find ways around obstacles

Deeper understanding of one's interests and passions as well as broader understanding of the world in general

EMPATHY, LEADERSHIP, TEAMWORK, RESILIENCE, PERSEVERANCE, COMMUNITY

The 20,000 Foot View

The image on the preceding page can be found online in a larger format here http://bit.ly/2ad0XBj.

Going into this project, we were all completely committed to doing something different for kids. Something we believed would make learning come to life in exciting ways for them - and for us. We were sure of one thing: we would give it 100%, document what happened, and then evaluate the program objectively to decide how to move forward.

It's not every day you can get a team of educators and leaders to dive in to something like this and consistently support it all the way through on faith and trust that it will work. Luckily, we had all of those things in place and that consistent support and dedication to the program's success made magic happen for kids.

The progression plan pictured on the preceding page details the basics of where our kids were when we started and where they were at the end of the year, with regard to basic life skills, such as emotional intelligence and social skills, as well as highly sought after professional skills, such as problem solving, collaboration, and leadership.

The strategic baby steps we took from day one, with open-ended play, to day 180, with an in depth and complex project, can be seen here, at a glance, in a way that visually reflects the day to day lessons which follow in the next chapter.

This is what created the foundation for a successful program which was relevant and engaging for *all* of our students.

This document didn't exist going in because we didn't know exactly what we were starting with and we had no way of knowing what the future would hold.

In creating it after the fact, we were able to put together an authentic representation of the year's progression and we are very pleased to be able to offer it to you, as yet another piece of your road map. Being able to see the program at-a-glance in conjunction with the nitty gritty detail will - we hope - give you everything you need to make amazing things happen for your kids.

> *The Maker philosophy: An approach to teaching that is built on a foundation of hands-on learning through building and making things. Learning is personal, passion driven and intrinsically motivated. Teachers are guides and mentors, not deliverers of curriculum.*

Progression Explained

At the top of the diagram, the wide bar and notes just below it represent an overview of the types of activities we offered and where the students were, socially, when we started. As you move to the right, you'll see where they were at the end of the year. The chart details how we cultivated the skills organizations and industry are looking for. Academics are great, but hiring managers are looking for more than that alone. They want young people who are capable of innovating and contributing in unique ways.

One of the challenges that many of our youth and young adults face today is the lack of ability to discuss their thoughts with others. We saw

25

this class as an opportunity to do something about this problem.

We started out talking to the students about the Maker philosophy and the idea that we are all better together. We explained the expectations of the class to them: be nice, help each other, share the things you've done, so others may benefit.

In the first days of this class, you could have heard a pin drop. The students were timid and shy. Not super-interested in talking to each other, or to us. By the end, they were a community, eager to get into groups, discuss their thoughts and ideas, and share with us about all of it.

Another challenge we see with young people is a lack of perseverance and resilience; a byproduct of our instant gratification culture. How do you address this in school? Make school a place kids *want* to be. A place that makes them feel alive and curious, and then couple that with access to tools, so they have an outlet for their newfound passion for learning.

How did we create that in the makerspace? We stealthily baby stepped our way into a world where our kids were no longer at "school;" they were in a place that gave them an opportunity to develop their own burning passion to create and to learn. A place where they were given the power to find their own personal connection to learning. That was the secret sauce in our recipe.

By starting out with short, student directed projects, we got them hooked on doing things. And the more they did, the more success they got to experience, which led to a stronger desire to keep diving further...to keep going. It was a cycle that quickly became fueled by the students themselves and at that point, we got to shift from cheering them on, to get started, to supporting them in their - sometimes lofty -

self-defined goals.

One critical element that stood out to us part way through the year was the feedback loop. Once we got students to a place where they felt safe in taking a risk (that took some serious doing) and trying something new, they would instantly - and briefly - feel an extreme sense of confidence and accomplishment. Acknowledging those moments and providing the external feedback with a quick, "hey, great job!" or similar compliment allowed them to continue building their confidence and their desire to re-enter the loop and take another chance on something new and more challenging.

> *Not noticing their moment of triumph can be devastating in these very vulnerable moments. This is one of the most important arguments to having time as the teacher to walk the class, notice what your kids are doing, and be there to empower, encourage and support when you are needed.*

It's not about diving in to do anything for them, it's about constantly giving them permission and encouragement to stay in their own driver's seat.

Striking the Proper Balance

Maker education programs have been implemented in a pretty wide range, from zero structure disasters to overly detailed "boxed" solutions, neither of which will create the environment kids need to truly have a life changing experience.

The structure we created for our class was definitely there, but mostly invisible; the most visible parts being the expectations we communicated and regularly reinforced:

Be kind
Create interesting things
Keep the space looking the way you found it when you leave
Be supportive of one another
Be inspired
Have fun

There's a very fine balance you have to strike to get this right. Seeing the progress made during Adventures in Making and how shy, disconnected students found meaning and inspiration alongside gregarious and academically successful students was proof for us that we struck that balance in a really great way for our kids.

Follow the essence of this plan and you will strike that balance for your kids too. You'll see them connect with learning in amazing ways and when you do, share your stories with the world to keep this work thriving and growing so even more can benefit from the magic of Making.

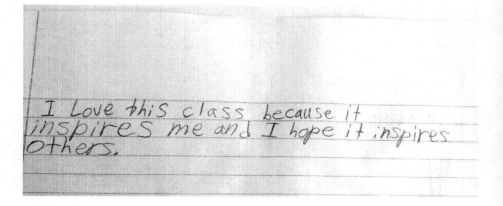

I Love this class because it inspires me and I hope it inspires others.

Grading for Success
(and productive failure)

It is absolutely imperative your students' motivation to do well in this class comes from within, not because they are being graded and measured. We can't stress this enough.

A couple years ago, in response to teacher after teacher asking how they could afford to integrate technology in their classroom when they were already so stressed teaching the "regular stuff" to be tested, I had a bold moment and blurted out, "Don't people realize the test is LIFE?"

That's why we're teaching kids. We're teaching them how to be successful in life, not to be good test takers. Those skills come, not from us telling kids what to do and requiring them to do it, but through giving them real opportunities to exercise choice, set goals, and define their own personal learning experience.

In a class such as this, where it's run as an elective and you aren't shouldered with the responsibility of teaching what will be tested, you have a unique opportunity to approach grading in ways that are empowering and healthy for your kids.

Phil's advice is to grade based on participation:

> If they were busy and making and on task that was 85% of their grade. The other 15% was how well they followed directions. For instance, when I had them detail out their plan for a project to submit to me, I would write a rubric on the board and they would follow that. They would also follow a rubric for reflective writing

and for presenting their finished projects.

Grading in this way allowed students to feel completely free to mess up, iterate their designs and take time getting their projects to a place they could be proud of. It also made the process much more equitable for the wide range of students we had in the class - from those who spoke broken English to those who were experienced inventors.

It was always about the process. Never about the product.

Another option (and one we are exploring this year) is allowing students to assess their own progress as a huge part of their grade.

Joy Kirr, National Board Certified ELA teacher, implemented this type of system in her class. She states on her blog that feedback was given in lieu of grades and that her students "gave themselves their final grade and grade-report comments each quarter, using proof."

What a fantastic way to further engage students! After all, it is their learning. Maybe the grades should be theirs too.

Here's an excerpt from her blog explaining her process:

- I was forthright with parents from the start. A letter went out the first week of school, and I updated parents with an email every two weeks.

- First quarter, we created a chart so students can fill it in with proof they've collected.

- We came up with myriad ways (and one central location) to prove our learning (this document is always changing).

- I began a document with comments I could copy and paste into the online grading system.

- We used a survey at midterm (which I've already edited for next year) for one check in.

- We discussed "effort," and how much impact that should or should not have on grades. Our final decision was to keep effort out of the grade. If students were putting in the effort, they should get the grade. One of the quotes students liked - "Don't be upset with the results you didn't get from the work you didn't do."

- I created sample examples of videos students could create to explain their grade.

- Students shared videos with me explaining their grade while providing proof. For students who did not prepare, or who did not develop this skill of reflecting in this way, I met with them one-on-one to come up with a final grade.

- Second Quarter, students in this class gave better feedback and quality boosters than my other classes. We also decided that the final pieces for proof did NOT have to be published. This is more fuel for making our writing more meaningful for students.

- I began giving video feedback - very valuable. I've learned how to use Explain Everything and Screen-cast-ify efficiently as a result.

- The first parent inquiry was about revisions - did her son HAVE to revise his writing? This was the catalyst for the Feedback Loop.

- All year, I felt like I was cheating my other classes who did not give themselves a grade at the end of each quarter. I have spent the first month of this summer excited that my other classes will be taking this trip with me this next school year!

Excellent!

She also received positive responses from the parents of her students:

- "I think that students have learned to reflect and improve more (w/teacher's help) minus the stress of 'grades.'"

- "Small amount of homework is great."

- "My son seems more interested in reading than recent years. If grading himself did that, then this approach was very successful."

- "When it comes to grading, while it is important, it's more important that the child is learning. Grades can be somewhat subjective so as long as the child is improving on the subject, being graded is second-ary."

- "Hopefully during the process the kids took more ownership of their results, they were always given a chance to correct, enhance or re-do - so if this happened grades should all be good."

- "My attitude towards the grading process has changed with the introduction of a collaborative process between teacher and student. Much like a class with a more 'traditional' grading system, students were given ample feedback on assignments from the teacher. What made this class unique, however, is that students were also given a sense of ownership in this process. It was no longer a one-way communication of grade from the teacher, but the process became a tool for ongoing engagement between the teacher and student. I would like to thank you, Mrs. Kirr, for covering not only the classics, but encouraging students to explore their individual interests. It is very apparent to us as parents that you love to teach and that you are expanding 'traditional' boundaries in an effort to encourage reading, critical thinking, and self-reflection. Thanks also to the administrators at Thomas and District 25 for supporting these new learning methods. We are grateful that ___ had the opportunity to participate in this process."

Even better!

Her feedback system coupled with students forming their own grades based on the structures she created for them was great for her kids, great for their families, and great for her as a teacher.

It doesn't really get any better than that.

Joy's resources and guidance are laid out very well on her websites, which I encourage you to visit. You can find her full post on feedback and grading for Genius Hour here: http://geniushour.blogspot.com/search/label/Grading and her class website, which is full of wonderful things that will save you time and inspire you here: http://scholarsrm239.weebly.com/.

So there it is, plain and simple. Approaching grading in this way removes so much of the stress students feel and truly equalizes the journey for all of them to achieve their personal best and take pride in the process and the results.

/may ker SPAY see an/

noun

"A special breed of human that proves you only need an imagination and a pile of junk to make anything a reality."
-Makerspace Ambassadors

180 Days of Lessons and Activities

The following pages contain all of the professional development, plans, activities, and notes our team used to create the Adventures in Making class.

Preparing for the Class

> *"Are you interested in robotics, creating state of the art films, graphic design or coding? Then the Adventures in Making class is for you! This newly designed class will allow students to explore a wide variety of high tech and low tech options in the world of making. Students will have the opportunity to be creative and innovative as they work on projects of their choice as well as real world projects that benefit our local community. Join us in the Makerspace for a year of fun and exploration!" (This is the description we used to promote enrollment for the class)*

As teachers breathing life into this new program, it would benefit you to watch this video before class: http://youtu.be/3Ml9j1UkeI4

You can ignore the fact that it's talking specifically about the organization (Maker Ed) and glean the parts that talk about supporting the Maker Movement and what it's all about. :-)

We didn't follow the normal professional development cycle in preparing the teachers for this class, in fact, we starting by telling them:

We are NOT going to teach this class!

This is how we introduced the philosophy behind Making and the plan for facilitating the experience. There were some serious sideways-eyed looks on this first day.

Oh yeah, and we also told them we were not giving homework. Ever.

A few weeks into the school year, the kids sheepishly asked about homework and the response was that we would never, ever give them homework in this class. We told them they could certainly work on things at home if they wanted to, but we would not impose that on them. It was their choice to make. You could literally feel the collective sigh of relief in the room.

We wanted the teachers to understand the paradigm shift we were asking them to make so we could get started on the right line of thinking straight away. This phrase was repeated more than once as we moved through the basics of what the class would look like.

We didn't do a lot of workshop time up front or long trainings where everything was explained in the beginning. Looking back, this was a risky move, but it paid dividends in the end because it allowed us to leverage "just in time learning" throughout the year with the teachers. This offered a much deeper and much more personalized approach to each moment where support was needed and it gave context to every single piece of their journey in Making.

Since we aren't able to offer that partnership in person to you, we offer it via the coach's notes and reflections you'll find throughout the lessons. We've done everything we can to capture the essence of those moments and conversations so you have them at your fingertips.

In addition, at the end of the book, you will find ways to reach out to us in case you have questions or need a little more support from us.

Phil (the P.E. teacher) gave this advice for other teachers in an online interview:

> *"Don't be afraid to just step back and watch. I remember you [Michelle] came in to one of the classes early in the year and that was your advice to me; 'step back and watch the magic happen,' and that was perfect. That's a huge thing, to be able to step back and let it happen, especially as a traditional classroom teacher, because that's not what you do. You have to be willing to step back and let them be noisy, let them struggle and figure things out. Being able to do that is very beneficial. This is where you get to see kids really dive in and work, and if you can do that, you're going to be just fine."*

In order to create a program that had the right scaffolding for the students (and the teachers), we detailed every step of the way in a manner that provided a broadly defined road map. This allowed us to give enough detail to support and guide, while also building in a ton of flexibility which allowed for teachers' personal style to be woven in.

In this class, kids aren't following a specific set of directions to create a set product. They are experimenting, being curious, making mistakes and adjustments, and discovering where their imagination can take them, individually and as members of a larger Maker community.

As the teacher, your challenge is to build a structure and culture around student voice. Your kids must be active participants in helping you to decide what their time in your classroom looks like.

> *You'll find great success in the progress of your students if you don't think of this as a "class you are teaching". .. instead, think of it as an environment where you are all learning together.*

Early on, the teachers said to me, "We don't know how to use all of the equipment and software in this room, how are we going to deal with learning about this mountain of stuff?" This was a fantastic opportunity to help them understand what it was all about as I got to tell them they didn't need to know how to do everything.

When a student asks you how to do something, you get to say, "I don't know, let's figure it out." It's about connecting kids with the learning resources that are all around them, from YouTube videos, to tutorials, and other Makers. You don't have to be the holder of knowledge, and when you can embrace that, it will be a truly liberating experience for you as a teacher.

Activities Explained

Each section begins with coach's notes, followed by the plans provided for running the class. We've concluded each section with our reflections on the activity, which is a critical piece of our learning we hope helps you to build on what we did in your own unique way.

Each lesson or activity follows a standard structure, which is:

DAY X-Y
TOPIC/ACTIVITY
OBJECTIVE(S)
COACH'S NOTES (where applicable)
FURTHER EXPLANATION
MATERIALS USED
REFLECTIONS (where applicable)

In addition, there are occasional **Do**, **Say**, **Discuss** and **Question** call-outs to draw your attention to specific pieces that will help you in guiding your class successfully. These taper off as the year progresses, as you'll get into the groove and it will become natural for you, without redundant reminders from us.

> *We've been really careful to not call this curriculum, for a lot of reasons, but mainly because we want to encourage you to make it your own and feel free to use this as a fluid plan that is meant to be changed and edited to fit your specific set of circumstances. This is especially true of the day to day list of activities.*

This documentation is meant to be a guide for you, not necessarily the singular way to make this happen with your kids. Feel free to venture off the path, incorporate your own ideas and, of course, find ways to make this work with the tools and equipment you have in your space. To make that even easier, we've also included open space at the end of each lesson for you to write in your own notes, edits, and changes. Go forth and conquer in your own unique ways!

As we share what we did on day 1 through day 180, keep in mind that some of these activities build on the previous ones, leading up to the Rube Goldberg challenge as the culminating project. They also build in time for brain breaks, iteration and productive failure as well as time around holidays and school breaks. So, as you head in, take a look at this in a way that allows you to create that same kind of flexibility for you and your students.

Allowing yourself and your kids the time to do things without the stress of "getting to the next piece of the lesson on time" will make all the difference in the world in the success (and joy) of your program.

A quick note about grouping

In our first year, we let the kids choose their own groups all the time. In reflecting, and reading lots of articles that talk about group dynamics, we as a team feel there is a balance you can strike with grouping that works better than always letting students choose. Our second year of this program will come with a few changes to how we group kids.

Giving your students the ability to choose is important as it empowers them and also gives them the sense of safety that is necessary to cultivate their ability to take risks and try new things. In year two of our Maker elective, we will begin the year with allowing students to choose their own groups and group sizes (within reason). As soon as we feel they are ready, we will also incorporate some guided grouping.

There are a ton of resources on the web on this particular topic, all with varying philosophies and research to back them up so we're not going to go in depth here, as you can find and use what works best for you.

Just be sure that, however you choose to group your kids, you balance the two worlds of choice and structure and reflect on how it works for your kids. Nothing is ever so good that it can't get better.

There are three forks in the road

One is the fork you travel because you have to, because someone in charge tells you that is the fork you take.

The second is the fork you take because someone in charge tells you it is good for you and you want to do "what is good for you."

Most kids in school today travel on one of the first two forks in the road. If they can't find a way to fit in there, sadly, many leave the road all together, only to find more challenges and struggles. Maker education offers *all kids* a third fork in the road. A choice that brings the full glory of meaningful learning into focus for every single child, regardless of ability, social background, gender or ethnicity.

The third is the fork you take because you are curious, or it is your passion, and you are personally and intrinsically motivated to travel that path, seeking out discovery. Discovery of yourself. Discovery of the world around you. Discovery of your passions and talents and how to turn those things into a future.

There is a huge difference between forcing students to show up to school, do their homework, learn the things they'll be tested on, and creating an environment conducive of allowing students to find their own motivation for learning. It's time to make the third fork in the road available and accessible to all through maker education.

Daniel Pink talks about this in his book *DRIVE*, Sir Ken Robinson touches on it in his book *The Element*, Simon Sinek talks about it in his book *Start with Why* as well as his TED Talk: How Great Leaders Inspire Action. Seth Godin talks about it, in essence, in all of his work.

> *The following activities are all about allowing students to see their own personal third fork in the road and empowering them to walk it.*

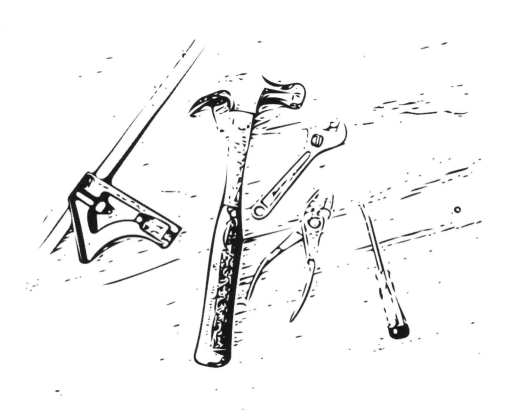

> *Important advice from Phil:*
> *"Be sure you look forward at least a*
> *couple weeks in advance to make sure*
> *you have the materials you need for the*
> *next project, so your students aren't*
> *waiting on orders to come in."*

DAY 1:

TOPIC/ACTIVITY:

Introduction to Adventures in Making, Maker philosophy and other student Makers.

OBJECTIVE(S):

1. Students gain an understanding of what the Maker Movement is and how it relates to: 1) students on an individual level and 2) students as a part of the larger community.

2. Students are introduced to the goals and expectations of the Adventures in Making class, including how grading will work.

3. Teacher(s) gain an understanding of student expectations through discussion.

Coach's Notes:

We entered the first day of school with 50 middle school students (in two separate classes) who had no idea what they were in for. We led the introduction to the class in both sessions and started out by telling all of them, "This class is going to be different. Your time in here is going to be amazing because it will be like nothing you've ever done before in school." Their faces revealed their thoughts loud and clear: "prove it."

After nearly a decade in "traditional school" we couldn't really blame them for their lack of enthusiasm. They were a tough crowd to get started with, but it didn't take long for us to win them over.

FURTHER EXPLANATION:

Open class with discussion:
Say: We are all going to "wade in" together in this class. We are going to try things together, support one another in exploring and learning new things.

Most importantly, we want you to have opportunities to explore many topics, and find activities that are interesting to you personally, whether it's art or coding, or something you didn't even know existed until you came here. We're here to give you the freedom and support you need to dive into those topics and learn more about them at your own pace. This class is structured so you can take that learning and create the products of your imagination.

Do: Introduce your students to the adventure they've signed up for. Let them know this is not going to be the usual class they're used to and, instead, it is an open environment for them to explore art, coding, robotics, engineering, filmmaking, graphic design, and more. It's a place to explore, to tinker and to create interesting things.

Show a video that reflects making, such as Maker Ed's "A Story of Why Making Matters:"
http://youtu.be/Yt1rjyKzX-E

Question: Ask your students open ended questions like, "What stood out to you?" or "Tell me something you're curious about after seeing this."

Discuss:

What is making?

What is a makerspace?

What is a Maker?

Question: Ask questions about students' expectations for the class.... What do they think this is going to be?

Do: Allow the class to be defined by the students, with minimal structure that is necessary for success.

Discuss: Overview of the class:

-- Starting with explore time where you can try out a variety of things, get to know what the possibilities are.

-- Dive into something you're interested in.

-- If there's interest we can also create things to be sold in the student store to fund purchase of more cool stuff for the makerspace.

-- Expectations: support each other, learn from each other, make interesting things, and HAVE FUN!

-- Reiterate (if necessary) how to be successful academically in this very different environment.

Say: We ask three things from you in this class:

Be supportive of one another.

Be curious.

Be creative.

Have FUN!

MATERIALS AND RESOURCES USED:

On this first day, we felt it was extremely important to give both students and teachers a visual of the stages of Maker learning, so everyone could see the easy entry point and where to go from there. We found an amazing resource in Jackie Gerstein, Ed.D., who published the following post on her blog titled Stages of Being a Maker Learner (https://usergeneratededucation.wordpress.com/2015/07/28/stages-of-being-a-maker-learner/ *reprinted with permission*):

> "So what is making? I've proposed that the heart of making is creating new and unique things. I also realize that in order for this type of making to occur, there needs to be some scaffolding so that maker learners can develop a foundation

of knowledge and skills. The end result, though should be maker learners creating new things by and for themselves. The ideas in this post have been sparked by the SAMR model. I see a similar pattern or progression with maker education:

Copy – make something almost exactly as someone else has done.

In this age of information abundance, there really is an unlimited number of DIY resources, tutorials, YouTube videos, online instructors and instructions on making all kind of things. These resources provide a good beginning for acquiring some solid foundational skills and knowledge for learning how a make something one has never made before.

Advance – gain more advance knowledge and skills by doing similar projects

During this stage, the maker learner, who desires to learn more about a given skill, project, or product, gains more advanced skills and knowledge by exploring additional and more advanced resources and by using these resources to create more advanced makes.

Embellish – add something that has been done; add a little of one's self to it.

When embellishing, maker learners extend their copied projects to include their own ideas. They tailor the copied projects to include their own ideas or embellishments. Example embellishments can be found with 3D printing, Makey-Makey, and littleBits adaptations.

Modify – take what others have done and modify or morph it into something new.

When modifying, maker learners take something that has been created before and tweak it to make something new. An example is the cardboard challenge where kids who were inspired by Caine's Arcade build their own cardboard creations.

Create – make or create something new, unique, different than what has been created before

When creating, maker learners create something unique or new. A simple example is when kids (and adults) take apart toys and use those parts to create new kinds of toys. A more complex example was the first folks who created prosthetic arms for 3-D printers.

Getting to Create stage will not occur for everyone but the Create doesn't have to be that unique or earth shattering. It just means making something – anything more different or unique than what has been made before. I do believe, though, that maker learners need to get beyond the Copy and Advance stages to add something of themselves to their makes. I believe this is what true making is all about."

She also created the following graphic, to illustrate the process and progression:

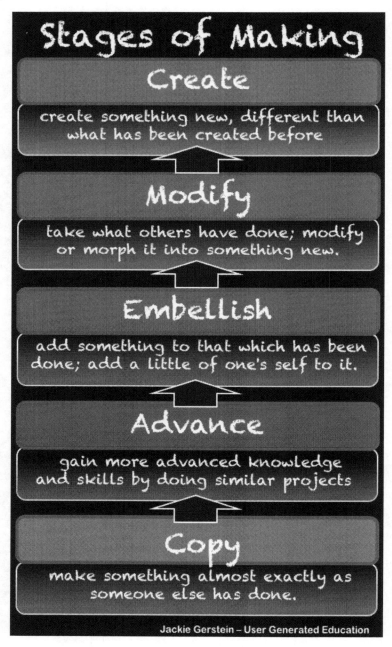

Coach's Notes:

Dr. Gerstein's work and her blog were a huge help in the process of creating our Maker elective class. This particular resource was especially helpful in guiding students to approach their experience with the mindset that they could start out by finding something they wanted to copy, because it was interesting to them, and they could take their own journey from there.

It was important on this very first day to begin developing these pieces straight away so that we all had something we could build on as we went through the year.

Do: let students know what's in store tomorrow: tinker time!

REFLECTIONS:

As a team, we felt our first day went really well. We launched the class, had great discussion and set everyone's expectations for what it would be and how success would be defined in this very new environment.

Looking back now, as the lead person developing this class, I can tell you that it was quite the wild adventure convincing everyone that it would be successful. My vision for what it was going to look like and how it would run was very different from what everyone was used to, and the lack of traditional structure and planning earned me quite a few "sideways eyes" from everyone as we headed into uncharted territory together.

Thankfully, the team trusted me enough to follow my lead, even though they didn't always see the end that I saw in clear view.

Day one, check. Plan for day two through day five, check. On we go!

From here on, you're going to see these little notepad pages at the end of each lesson. Use them to jot down your own thoughts, lesson tweaks, etc.

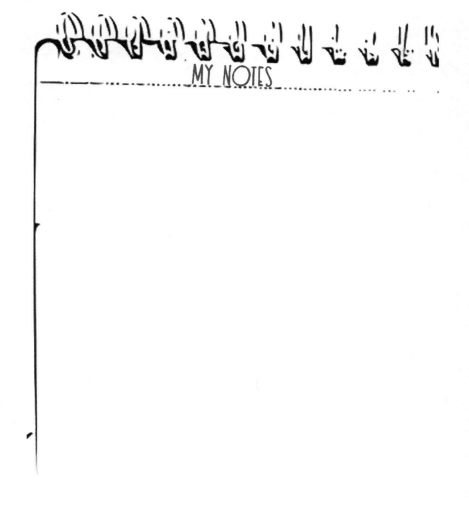

MY NOTES

DAY 2-5:

TOPIC/ACTIVITY:

Exploration of supplies and equipment / tinker time

OBJECTIVE(S):

1. Students will explore and become aware of all of the tools and supplies available to them in the class.

2. Class culture continues to be developed.

Coach's Notes:

Between the students not believing this class would be different, the teachers being uncomfortable heading in somewhat blind, and more power in the hands of the students, these days were a challenge, but it turned out to be the best thing we could have done to start out on the right foot in this class.

If you're coming from a traditional classroom background, or simply aren't used to having unstructured time, these days will be hard, but they are necessary in getting students to come out of their shell and begin building the confidence they will need to try more difficult projects along the way.

FURTHER EXPLANATION:

If your school or district has a coach, curriculum support provider or other support staff, it's helpful to have the extra set of hands in your class, at least part of the time for this activity.

Say: You're going to have 2-3 days to explore all of the tools available to you in the classroom. That means you can check out what's in the cabinets, use the computers, iPads, etc. We want this to be a time for you to discover, try things, and have fun getting to know what's in here.

Do: Set clear expectations. Let students know that if they take something out, they need to be sure and make a note of how and where they found it. Everything has a place and it goes back in the same condition you found it - organized, neatly packed, etc.

Say:

Remember to:
Be supportive of one another.
Be curious.
Be creative.
Have FUN!

Question: Are there any questions before we let you get started?

Now let them go and explore the room.

Coach's Notes:

Depending on your kids, you may have to let them know this time is to explore the supplies in the class, not funny videos of cats or on-line games. In this particular class, we didn't have to do that, but in other places this was necessary to keep things on track.

Setting expectations up front is a much more effective method of classroom management than dealing with issues as they arise. Not setting expectations up front will definitely lead to students doing things they aren't supposed to, and when you have to call them on it, the dynamic can turn rapidly to one centered on power struggles and loss of positive inspiration.

Do: Cruise your classroom and guide students where necessary. Notice what they gravitate towards. Give them tips about online learning tools related to what they're tinkering with. This will enable them to continue successfully pursuing learning on their own.

For example, we had iMacs loaded with Adobe Creative Suite software and we let students know about the tutorial videos linked to each program, in case they wanted to know more about how to use those programs. If you have a 3D printer, tell students about the free online design tool tinkercad.com and the built in tutorials.

> *Remember that the responsibility to learn is in their hands. If you come upon a student who needs you to tell them how to do something, redirect them to resources they can access on their own to learn. This relates directly to the comment I opened our first teacher PD with: "We are NOT going to teach this class. We are going to teach students how to learn by empowering them."*

Coach's Notes:

One of the things that I've learned through years of working with and interviewing students, especially at-risk youth, is that expectations which are set too high right out of the gate can stifle or even paralyze a student's ability to try new things. Add the stress of a class full of middle schoolers nervous about how they look to their peers, and you're ability to get them comfortable gets even trickier.

This open-ended tinker time - coupled with absolutely no expectation to produce - is exactly what students need to venture out of their comfort zone and begin developing relationships with one another that will come in handy later on as we add complexity and depth to the projects.

A principal said something once that rings true in this situation: "Students in their natural environment are completely different than they are at school. They talk and have ideas and are naturally curious beings."

This is the environment we are creating in these first few days. An environment where students feel like they can be present, be themselves and be a part of school in a way that breathes new life into learning for them.

It will feel awkward for everyone for the first day or two. That is normal. Allow it to happen. Allow it to become the wonderful environment you need to move forward to the next activity.

Do: End with a video to spark imagination and show your students how totally open their road is:
Caine's Arcade: http://youtu.be/faIFNkdq96U

Discuss: Talk about the video using open ended questions that get the students thinking and sharing out loud. (For example, "What comes to mind after watching this?")

Do: Let students know they have more tinker time tomorrow.

Coach's Notes:

At the end of the first day of this activity, I walked in to the classroom to find the teacher frustrated trying to get the students to begin cleaning up. They were so engrossed in what they were doing that it was difficult to pull them away.

Immediately, I remembered something I had seen a teacher do in her class a few years before and I knew would make this cleanup process much easier and more fun for everyone:

Implement a cleanup system using something similar to this clip of the Mission Impossible music, which you can find on YouTube. There are a ton of different versions, and we used one that was several minutes long. We told the students that from that day on, when they heard the music start, it was time to put things away and clean up. It worked like a charm! We never again had trouble getting them to clean up and we didn't have to try and talk over them to get their attention.

From Phil:

"When talking about clean up time, I found it better to give more time than you'd think you need. That way, when all is cleaned up you can talk and debrief with the class. If you run out of time before that then you can also talk the next day."

MATERIALS AND RESOURCES USED:

The materials you need for this activity will depend entirely on what you have in your makerspace. For a list of all the resources, tools, and supplies we used, you can refer to our equipment and supply list which is in the back of this book and also online here: http://bit.ly/29tGqqL

REFLECTIONS:

My biggest a-ha moments after this first week were related to how uncomfortable it was for students and teachers to enter into this very different world. It was important for me to be clear, kind, and most of all, present and supportive in order to keep them on board and trusting in the process.

From Phil:

"This was huge for the kids and myself. Absolutely necessary. They got to see a lot of things that they would get to be doing throughout the year, and the excitement was uncontrollable."

DAY 6-7

TOPIC/ACTIVITY:

Maker Notebooks

OBJECTIVE(S):

1. Each student will create their own personalized Maker notebook for use in sketching, planning, documenting and reflecting on ideas and projects.

Coach's Notes:

Rather than giving students a ready made notebook, we gave them cardboard, various kinds of paper, access to punches and paper cutters and let them first build their book, bind it, then decorate it.

Letting students create and then artsy up their books is an important piece in getting them to feel a sense of ownership and pride in the book and what they will be putting into it as the class unfolds.

FURTHER EXPLANATION:

Say: As makers, it's important that we share our work with others. Sharing is a fundamental piece of being a maker and inspiring others to make things. Here's a quick video to show the power of documenting and sharing: http://youtu.be/V4DDt30Aat4

Discuss: Think of a time when you used someone's documentation to help you accomplish something you wanted to do. Share with class. (could be a how-to video for something in Minecraft, fixing your bike, etc.)

Do: Give students an overview of what they will be using the notebooks for and some basic parameters such as final overall size and how many sheets of paper they should include.

To start the documentation process, every Maker should have a notebook. Your notebook is your place to jot down ideas, sketch things you might want to fabricate later, doodle, reflect, etc.

In addition, each entry will also include the following, which becomes part of each students participation points:

1. Pitch / idea

2. Sketches / drawings / plans

3. Notes about challenges and revisions

4. Notes about how your group worked together

5. Reflections from group conversations

Say: Let's create and personalize our Maker notebooks!

Step 1: take two pieces of cardboard for the front and back cover. Decorate with your choice of embellishments, make sure your name is proudly displayed, etc.

Step 2: Collect various types of paper: plain, lined, graph, colored, etc. Put all papers together and mark where you need to cut to size and where holes need to be punched.

Step 3: Binding! Cut three strings in your choice of color and tie LOOSELY through each hole. You can do bows if you want to be able to untie and add more paper later or knots if you want it to be permanent.

Coach's Notes:

There are more complex ways to bind books and if you have the tools and the desire to explore those options, go for it! If you're unsure, what we've offered here is the easy way to bind your books.

Discuss: At the end of each day, allow 5-10 minutes for sharing, questions and discussion about the process of creating the books, ideas, challenges, etc.

MATERIALS AND RESOURCES USED:

- Cardboard for front and back cover

- Various types of paper: lined, graph, blank, etc.

- Yarn or cord to bind

- Duct tape, washi tape, glitter, paint, etc. to decorate

The Maker notebook is step one in the documentation process and serves as the rough draft for what students will be posting on their websites. The following document, produced by Maker Education Initiative details more on the topic of documentation (used with permission):

http://makered.org/wp-content/uploads/2015/02/OPP_ResearchBrief3_DIYDocumentationToolsForMakers_final.pdf

This document offers some wonderful information and explanation of the following:

• Unique challenges of Maker documentation

• Capturing with phones and tablets

• DIY solutions for Maker documentation

• Discussion and future steps

REFLECTIONS:

The notebook activity was great because it was our first opportunity to see individual and collective creativity come to life in the class. It was also another quick-return activity which was only mildly challenging and very gratifying for the students to work on. This was an important piece in continuing to build their resilience, and ability to sustain through longer more challenging projects.

We began to see each student's individual style through this activity, which was really helpful in building relationships with the class as a whole as well as each individual student.

"Notebooks are especially helpful for putting down what is happening inside their heads. Training the kids to track their progress and ideas."
~ Noelle

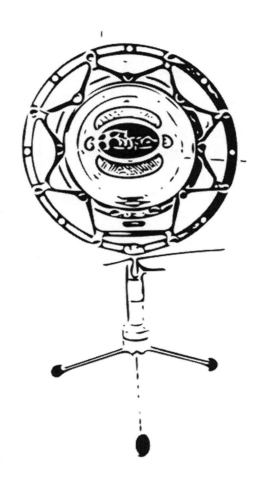

MY NOTES

DAY 8-9

TOPIC/ACTIVITY:

A short, introductory challenge in filmmaking and engineering, which builds teamwork, planning and communication skills.

OBJECTIVE(S):

1. Students get comfortable with making a choice, with only two or three options.

2. Students use their knowledge and comfort with the tools in the room to produce something.

3. Students use their new notebooks to sketch, document and reflect.

Coach's Notes:

This is purposeful in that many times students cannot make choices with open ended options in the beginning. This is something that needs to be scaffolded, starting out with asking them to choose from just a couple of options and working up from there.

FURTHER EXPLANATION:

NOTE: This activity runs for two days. Don't tell students about the instant replay tomorrow until the end of class. This is meant to happen twice in it's entirety.

Students will create three stations: one for demolition (building catapults that will demolish towers), one for engineers (to build the strongest towers) and one for filmmakers (to document all of the work happening around them).

Discuss: Take about 5 minutes to explain the activity to the class. Discuss and answer questions, if needed.

> *Remember, students have access to the Internet for plans, pictures, and how-to sites. They will not need anything beyond that - no worksheets, printed plans, instructions, etc. It's up to the students to find plans and execute them using the supplies they have access to.*

Do: Let students know they can choose one of the three stations. If they choose to start at demolition and decide it's not for them, they are welcome to move to a different station until they find the right "fit."

Coach's Notes:

You might be wondering if we had issues with students just roaming because we gave them the option to try and change stations until they found the right one. We did not have any trouble with this, which kind of surprised me at the time too. I wanted to put them in charge of making a good choice, but also wanted to give them the freedom to change their mind if they needed to. We had a few students try one or two stations at the beginning of class, but once they settled into the one they liked, they stayed there and were very productive.

Sometimes, giving students the power to choose empowers them just enough in class to get them engaged in the activity.

Students must choose a group and follow the instructions below:

The demolition group builds catapults, using resources on the Internet to research how to build and then GO! Depending on the size of your class, you may have more than one group building these, which is great, because they can then try out multiple designs to see which is most effective and accurate.

The engineers build towers using Keva Planks or similar material - the tallest, strongest towers they can build.

The filmmakers learn iMovie on the run and then begin filming the process and activities of the other two groups. (We offered a 5 minute tutorial to explain iMovie to get them started and the rest was up to them)

Culminate with the demolition group launching small objects at the towers using their catapults, while the filmmakers capture the whole thing on video, which is easily turned into a short documentary and uploaded to YouTube.

Coach's Notes:

This activity is a good high speed warm up - don't tell them it's going to take two days so they have a sense of urgency to get it done. At the end of the day, ask if they'd like to do it again tomorrow so they can perfect their process.

MATERIALS AND RESOURCES USED:

- Keva Planks

- iPads

- Craft sticks

- Rubber bands

- Tape

REFLECTIONS:

This was an exciting day for all of us, but especially for me. It was the first day I got the sense that I was beginning to get some real buy-in from everyone, students included.

When I share this story, most people look at me in amazement when I tell them we accomplished all of this in a 45 minute class of middle schoolers. We did. The sense of pride the students had in their work and their attention to detail on their projects was extremely inspiring for all of us. It was in this moment that we all began to see this was the beginning of an incredible journey that would change everything for these kids.

When we asked them if they'd like to go for round two the following day, we got a resounding "yes" from the whole class. They were hooked!

MY NOTES

DAY 10-18

TOPIC/ACTIVITY:

Sharing our work through student websites

OBJECTIVE(S):

1. Students create their own individual websites to showcase their work.

Coach's Notes:

It's very important to recognize that the creation of student websites is not just an assignment for your kids to complete. In order to produce the intended outcome, which is creating a space for them to share their work, reflect on their journey and receive positive and encouraging feedback from a larger community of Makers, the focus must be on creating something that is personally engaging for each individual kid. It has to be theirs.

Success will come from you consistently encouraging your kids to use their websites to share the cool stuff they're making with family and friends as well as other classes of Makers out in the world. The more real and connected you can make this activity, the more it will become a place for your kids to post and share their work enthusiastically.

FURTHER EXPLANATION:

Each student will be creating a Google Site (or other similar free website tool such as Wix, Weebly, etc) to showcase their projects, share what they're doing in class with others (such as relatives, community members, etc). This project reinforces the practice of students documenting and sharing their Maker projects with a broader audience.

Do: Share sample student sites to give your class some examples to use for inspiration. Here are a couple of examples from our Maker friends in Santa Rosa:

* http://cjanssen34ahs19.wix.com/cjmake#!project-blog/yc2ed

* http://bentheonein3rdperiod.wix.com/bensblog

* http://quinotopia.wix.com/quinotopia

Discuss: Your expectations for what will be included on their sites, how to get started, how much time they will have to complete this activity.

We used Google Sites. Here are the steps we took to get them started:

Noelle's Notes:

I gave the kids a quick tutorial on how Google Sites works. I then created a spreadsheet and had them put their name and the link to their site, that way Phil had access to them. You don't want all of the kids sharing their sites with you, because then you are stuck with a million sites forever.

I talked to them about design and fonts and things that real website designers have to think about. Then we let them go. Phil had them project their sites and share them at the end of the project, which worked out really well.

Step 1: Students will log into their google account and create a new site. Teachers should discuss naming conventions with students if you want them to have a specific format.

Step 2: Design and content: Students will have a few days to design their site and get it looking the way they want. It would be good to suggest the use of "how to" videos and class experts if they need help figuring out how to customize their site.

Sites will have the following pages and content:

- Homepage with a "welcome to my site" sort of message

- A "My Projects" page. This page will feature a running list of student projects, with photos, descriptions, videos, etc.

- An "About Me" page. On this page, students will follow the activities outlined in week 1 of the student blogging challenge. (http://bit.ly/2aK1zlj)

- An "Ideas for Later" page. Students should put at least one thing here that they'd like to make or tinker with sometime this year during their makerspace class.

Discuss: At the end of each day, allow for 5-10 minutes to discuss progress, challenges and triumphs. When questions come up from students about how to do something, allow the support to come from other students who have figured things out, rather than attempting to answer questions yourself.

MATERIALS AND RESOURCES USED:

Feel free to use whatever website system (or systems) you and your students are comfortable with. We used Google Sites because we are a Google Apps school, and also because this tool gave us a little more control over who could see and comment on students' sites.

Students will also use their own notes they've collected in their notebooks, as well as photos and videos they've taken of their projects, to populate their sites with initial content.

REFLECTIONS:

I read a student's account of how she felt when her teacher used her work to share out with colleagues because she had done something above and beyond. She said it made her feel like her work was important and useful beyond just the gradebook and because of that it made her strive to do better work. This is really impactful and pretty easy to do in this venue. Student websites will make it easy for us to share their work with colleagues and supports the idea that their work is valued.

MY NOTES

DAY 19-21

TOPIC/ACTIVITY:

Website presentations

OBJECTIVE(S):

1. Students gain familiarity with the qualities and characteristics of engaging presentations

2. Students begin to develop their own style and comfort with presenting to groups

Coach's Notes:

From the Mayo Clinic: "Fear of public speaking is a common phobia. It can range from slight nervousness to paralyzing fear and panic. Many people with a fear of public speaking avoid public speaking situations altogether, or they suffer through them with shaking hands and a quavering voice. But with preparation and persistence, you can overcome your fear."

Helping students to overcome their fears of public speaking early on can have a tremendous impact on their success as adults. Their first attempt at presenting in front of the class should be framed in a way that is enjoyable and supportive.

At this point, your students should have the beginning of a strong

and supportive team environment where everyone is rooting for their peers.

FURTHER EXPLANATION:

Students will present their websites, talk about design and content, where they got inspiration, and allow time at the end of their presentation for questions from the audience.

Because this was the first attempt at getting up in front of the group, we decided to add an additional element to make it fun and engaging by doing modified Ignite presentations.

If you're unfamiliar with this particular style, it is a format where presentations are limited to 5 minutes in length, with 20 slides total. The length is determined by setting the slides to advance automatically every 15 seconds.

Do: Before presentations begin, share a few examples of quality Ignite talks. A search of YouTube will give you plenty of options to choose from.

Discuss: Ask open ended questions and allow for class discussion following each example.

Students will use their Maker notebooks to take notes, if they choose, and will map out their outline here as well.

MATERIALS AND RESOURCES USED:

- Projector

- Screen

- Students' individual websites

REFLECTIONS:

There was one particular female student who was especially shy in our class. She sat there with her hair covering most of her face while she worked and when we announced that we'd be doing this activity, I could see the sheer terror in her eyes.

I remember being that kid. The one who would absolutely die if the teacher called on me in class, and I'd rather have failed everything than be made to speak in front of my peers.

When we were done explaining the activity, I knelt down by her chair and told her a little of my story about being terrified to stand up and speak. How it would give me the cold sweats and make my legs feel like spaghetti. I couldn't even speak from my desk. I followed it with, "and look at me now. I can speak in front of your class, or thousands of people and it's really fine." Her eyes opened wide and she said, "really?"

The whole exchange only took a few minutes, but it helped her see it in a different way. I acknowledged that her fear was real and listened to her. She did a fantastic job when it was her turn and I was so proud of her.

This is a scary thing to do and sometimes all it takes is saying that out loud, showing genuine empathy and then helping kids build their personal toolbox of things they can use to make it a little less scary. From there, everything gets easier.

> *From this point forward, students should incorporate taking photos, videos, and jotting down notes into their normal process for each activity. Where it fits and you feel it's appropriate for your class, be sure and include the process of adding their documentation to new posts on their websites.*

What I like about this is that you have the chance to unleash your imagination and to use that imagination to create something amazing,

MY NOTES

DAY 22-37

TOPIC/ACTIVITY:

Our first peek at a longer challenge: Create something interesting

OBJECTIVE(S):

1. Students become familiar with the concept of a pitch

2. Students develop teamwork, planning, and organization skills

3. Students further develop presentation skills

Coach's Notes:

This big project is broken up into three phases:

Phase 1: The pitch (2 days)

Phase 2: Creating the product (8 days)

Phase 3: Preparing presentations and presenting (6 days)

Be sure to remind your students to document their work as they go with sketches, notes, ideas, resources used, etc. This will make their website updates much easier.

Do be sure to discuss the overview of this project with students on the first day, so they are aware of the process and expectations from beginning to end.

Do: Allow students to form groups of 2-3 per group

Coach's Notes:

We purposefully did not choose groups for students here. To continue allowing them to build community and a supportive environment, as well as to continue developing their comfort level with the class and taking risks, we wanted them to choose partners and groups they felt would work well for them. We also wanted to give them the opportunity to make structured choices around the size of their groups.

Continuing to build on student choice and empowerment was a major factor in the successes we had in our class.

Phil adds:

"This was a <u>huge</u> contributor to success. The students, for the most part, got to choose what they wanted to explore and work on. That gave them ownership and a sense of pride."

FURTHER EXPLANATION:

PHASE 1:

Say: You will spend today and tomorrow developing a "pitch" for a project your group would like to work on for the next week and a half.

Discuss: What is a pitch?

Pitches should include the following:

1. What is your project in one sentence (i.e. "I'd like to create a LEGO movie." or "We'd like to develop a logo for this class.")

2. Why did you choose this project?

3. What tools do you need?

4. How is your team going to accomplish this task by the deadline?

The pitches will be given to the teacher on the third day for approval (If your class is especially gregarious, students can give the pitch to the entire class.)

Noelle shared Piktochart as a fun way for students to create their pitches. This free tool has some fun templates for making infographics. I've included the example she created on the next page. You can also find it online here: http://bit.ly/2ahmd9M

She also suggests that you try having students pitch projects to each other. They can then ask questions and help each other refine their projects, get feedback and expand on their ideas before pitching to you.

Do: Roam the class and connect with students who are ready to pitch their idea. Once you have determined the pitch details a viable (or possibly viable) project, giving that group a green light to get started.

Coach's Notes:

Your job is to listen to the pitch in a way that is supportive of student ideas and voice. Help them, if necessary, with holes in their plan, details, etc. Keep in mind the plan does not have to be perfect to

proceed. This is students' chance to have an idea and see it forward, experiencing the joy of success and accomplishment even when there might be bumps in the road or small failures along the way.

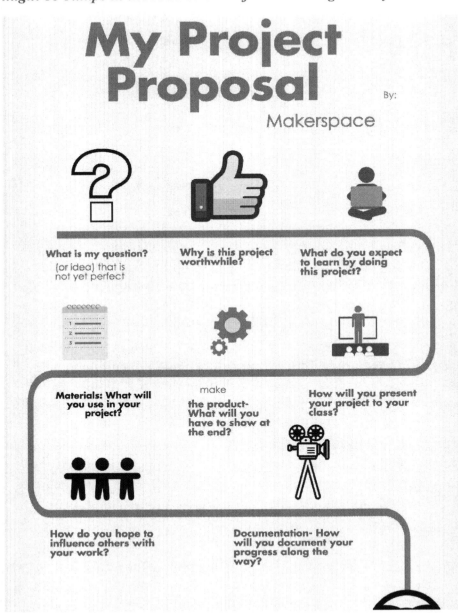

86

PHASE 2:

Students will have about 8 days to work on their project.

Discuss: Save about 5-10 minutes at the end of each day for reflection and sharing in a whole group discussion format.

PHASE 3:

For fun, we called the opening to this part "screamin' awesome presentations." (We spend 1-2 days on this section)

To give students an understanding of what makes a good presentation (and what makes a presentation awful or boring), we watched some TED Talks that fit into the categories of "great", "meh", and "terrible."

Here's an example of one of my all time favorite TED Talks:

> Simon Sinek, How Great Leaders Inspire Action
> (https://www.ted.com/talks/simon_sinek_how_great_leaders_inspire_action)

This talk is compelling, inspiring, and extremely informative, so it serves as one of the most perfect examples of what "great" looks like.

Phil adds:

"Although there are some fantastic TED Talks out there, I found that the ones that come from kids their own age resonated much more with them. They related to speaker better."

Here is a great Google doc students can use to help guide their preparation: http://ow.ly/HyAE302thh3 (graciously provided by Lisa Highfill and the folks over at Teachers Give Teachers)

Discuss: As a class, discuss what was great and what wasn't about the TED Talks. What stood out to your students? What do they want to incorporate into their own presentations?

NEXT:

Preparing your own screamin' awesome presentation. Now that students have a good idea of what works and what doesn't, they will have 2-3 days to prepare their own presentations, which will follow these guidelines:

- Introduction of group

- Overview of project and pitch

- Demonstration or sharing of finished project

- What challenges did they face and how did they overcome them?

NEXT:

Show us what you've got kids!

Groups will present their projects to a respectful and supportive audience over the next couple of days.

Discuss: Take about 3-5 minutes at the end of class for students to discuss, share and reflect as a group.

MATERIALS AND RESOURCES USED:

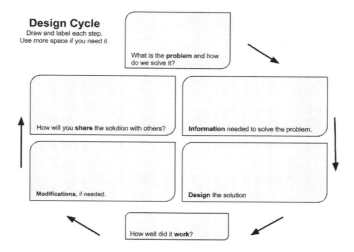

Noelle created a great document to help guide the students through the design cycle. They used this document throughout the year on all kinds of activities, including this project, mapping out presentations, reflections in their notebooks. You can find it online here: http://bit. ly/2aqA4d1

Other materials will depend entirely on the projects or products students choose to create during this activity.

We asked our classes to utilize existing resources for their projects, but also offered to purchase supplies if they were inexpensive and easily attainable.

REFLECTIONS:

At this point, Noelle, who had been with the class pretty regularly, noted that it was time for a brain break. She suggested we build in some team building activities that would allow the students to break from the intense process they just finished. This turned out to be a very successful and necessary addition to the class plan, and from this day on, it became a standard pause between big projects. Thanks Noelle!

MY NOTES

(Sketch provided by Jackie Gerstein of User Generated Education, https://usergeneratededucation.wordpress.com/)

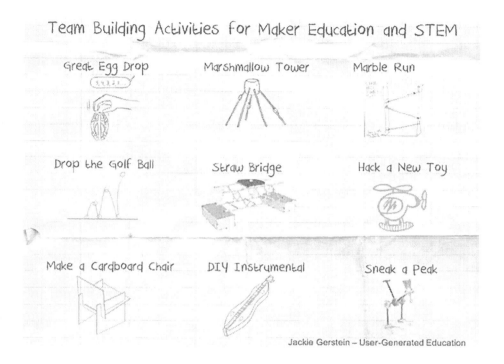

Team Building Activities for Maker Education and STEM

Great Egg Drop   Marshmallow Tower   Marble Run

Drop the Golf Ball   Straw Bridge   Hack a New Toy

Make a Cardboard Chair   DIY Instrumental   Sneak a Peak

Jackie Gerstein – User-Generated Education

DAY 38-43

TOPIC/ACTIVITY:

Reflection, feedback, and a brain break

OBJECTIVE(S):

1. Students reflect on their journey and learning thus far through a short writing activity

2. Students offer feedback to teachers and coaches that will help continue building the program in a true student centered way

3. Students build resilience through the process of working hard followed by a period of mental rest

Coach's Notes:

I recently read a great article in Harvard Business Review, written by Shawn Achor and Michelle Gielan which talks about resilience and how to cultivate this skill. The title alone, Resilience Is About How You Recharge, Not How You Endure, speaks volumes on the topic.

There are some people who will walk into your class during these brain break moments and ask you where the rigor is or some other similar question. The above mentioned article is research based back-up for the critical importance of these moments. These are the moments that give your students what they need to be successful, as students in your class and as adults.

When you get to the brain break, talk about the importance of rest with your students and what it does to help them achieve at higher levels.

> **Here's a real-life example of this...**
>
> **As I sit here writing this book, nearing the end of a very intense project, I am absolutely employing these principles as I work. I have made an agreement with myself to finish a section, and then break to spend a few minutes outside in my yard.**
>
> **It's amazing what we can accomplish when we allow ourselves to indulge in this cycle of intensely hard work followed by a period of rest or something that is just for fun.**

FURTHER EXPLANATION:

Kickoff the week with a "let us know what you think" writing prompt: (1-2 days)

Students will answer the following two questions:

1. What did you LOVE about the activity we just finished?

2. What suggestions do you have to make it better next time? OR What would you like to see as the next challenge? (The second part of this question was in place to help us create this plan. Now that the plan is done and you're reading it here, you can choose to ask that question of your students and edit the next activity accordingly.)

NEXT:

Follow up writing prompt with a brain break. Pick a team building challenge of your choosing, either from the following list, or something else you feel will best suit your class.

Dr. Gerstein's blog User Generated Education once again served as an invaluable resource to us here. Her post titled, "Team Building Activities That Support Maker Education, STEM, and STEAM" was full of great ideas that we used throughout the year.

Team Building Activities:

- Search Pinterest for "Engineering challenges with Keva Planks"

- Marshmallow challenge

- Straw bridge building

- Dr. Gerstein's list: http://bit.ly/2aK2BO3

- Bridge building hyperdoc (compliments of Noelle and Teachers Give Teachers): http://ow.ly/krkc302rVlN

- Mystery build challenges (compliments of Noelle) http://bit.ly/29ZW9B3 | http://bit.ly/2auF7KF | http://bit.ly/2ahk1yK

Discuss: Take about 3-5 minutes at the end of class for students to discuss, share and reflect as a group.

Coach's Notes:

These two activities can either fit into a week or can flow out into the following week, depending on how the classes take to them and what your observations are. Don't cut students short if they are engaged in creating the supportive team culture we're looking for. Use your good teacher judgment to decide.

MATERIALS AND RESOURCES USED:

- Maker notebooks

- Materials required for your chosen team building activity

REFLECTIONS:

Things were really starting to work well at this point. The teachers were seeing the purpose and rhythm of the activities and the students were amazingly engaged, committed and energized.

It was at about this point in the class that I created the following YouTube video to share with district and school leaders, as well as the school board: https://youtu.be/1puiorM9zwo

Phil shared some of the things he was hearing from his kids, including statements that they "wished they didn't have to leave this class."

> *You know you're doing something right when your kids create their own challenging work that incorporates both academic and life skills and they no longer see it as school, but a place they want to stay and keep working.*

There were several spontaneous reflective writing activities we did throughout the year, just to check in and give students an opportunity to give us both named and anonymous feedback. Every time, our hearts were warmed by the things we got to read from the kids. It was yet another way for us to surface their voices and ensure we were continuing to build the class around them.

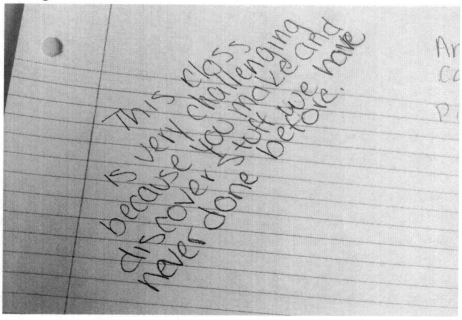

MY NOTES

DAY 44-69

TOPIC/ACTIVITY:

Product design and development via TWO options (students will choose one):

1. Design a product to sell in the student store (ideas: note cards, stickers, bookmarks or things made from duct tape) Teachers: feel free to fill in other options here and be open to ideas from your kids.

2. Design a product you think would be useful or interesting that you will not reproduce for sale. (i.e. cell phone projector)

OBJECTIVE(S):

1. Students further hone research and development (R&D) skills

2. Building perseverance, teamwork and presentation skills

3. Begin to develop an understanding of R&D work in industry

Coach's Notes:

This activity is very similar to the one we did during days 22 through 37, but with added complexity and additional opportunities for students to make choices.

Additionally, this activity allows students critical opportunities to iterate and improve, building their self confidence and self efficacy.

Noelle adds: "I think it would be fun for students to make short commercials for the products they have created. This could be a fun and different way to present their second project - and teach some new tech skills at the same time.

I like the idea of mixing it up and this concept can be used in several places following this activity.

> **As David Beach, Mechanical Engineer in Stanford's Product Realization Lab states in the video used here as a provocation moment, this process "...ignites the joy of making things. Students fail, learn, try again, do a little better, learn some more, try again..."**

FURTHER EXPLANATION:

For this activity, students can choose to work in groups, or individually.

Coach's Notes:

I gave them full authority to choose the size of their groups and their group members, telling them only that I didn't want to see half the class in one group. Another risk that paid dividends with our kids. They knew they were entrusted with the responsibility to make good decisions and they honored it with doing just that.

Know your kids. Trust them. Set clearly defined -and high - expectations and chances are they will not let you down.

The challenge:

Say: We are going to dive deeper into the process of imagining, designing and producing a product.

Watch this video as a provocation moment at the beginning of class: https://youtu.be/maS6Tn6cGi8

Say: You will spend this week researching ideas and developing a "pitch" for a product you'd like to create (either for the student store OR something using the materials and supplies in the makerspace.

Your pitch should include the following:

1. What is your product in one sentence?

2. Who is your audience? (Who might buy your product?)

3. IF making a product for the student store, how much will it cost you to produce your product? For example, if you are making note cards, how much does it cost to produce one? You will probably need some help from your teachers for this part.

4. How much will you sell your product for?

5. What is your profit?

6. What tools and/or supplies do you need?

7. Who is in your group, or are you working solo?

This part should look familiar:

Teachers: our job is to listen to the pitch in a way that is supportive of student ideas and voice, help them if necessary with holes in their plan, details, etc. Keep in mind the plan does not have to be perfect to proceed. This is the students' chance to have an idea and see it forward, experiencing the joy of success and accomplishment even when there might be bumps in the road or small failures along the way.

Once you have determined the pitch details a viable (or possibly viable) project, give groups a green light to get started.

Discuss: Talk about this activity as a class. Remind students that items made for the student store will be a way for them to make money and fund purchases for their makerspace.

Coach's Notes:

The further we go in the year, the less explanation students need to get started on projects. We maintained a consistent and clearly defined program, which allowed us to spend less time up front talking and more time encouraging while students create.

We had approval from district leadership to sell items in the student store, which made this all work very well. If you don't have a student store or don't have approval to do this type of activity, there are other ways you can run this, such as selling in a local shop owned by someone who is supportive of your program or selling in a "bake sale" type of format after school.

As in the previous pitch to product activity, you will allow students ample time for creating their products, followed by about 4 days of presentations.

In preparation for presentations:

Discuss: What students liked about their presentations from last time and what they want to do better this time.

MATERIALS AND RESOURCES USED:

Just as before, materials will depend entirely on what students choose to do. Also, as before, we asked them to stick with what we had as much as possible and offered to purchase additional items that were easy to get and inexpensive.

REFLECTIONS:

I have a story that came out of this activity that absolutely made my day:

One group decided that they would make homemade chalk in the shape of stars to sell in the student store. They found a recipe online and made their first batch. I happened to be at the school right after this to do some video work and I saw the girls outside at a table work-ing on their chalk product, hands covered in corn starch and having a great time.

On the pavement all around the table where they were working were inspirational phrases written in their homemade chalk that read things like "be inspired" and "be happy" with a smile drawn under the two "p's"

I walked over and started asking them questions about their project and one of the girls told me the recipe they found made chalk that worked, but when it dried, it cracked, making look less appealing. She said they discovered, by adding corn starch to the recipe, the chalk looked and worked better.

When I asked her how they figured that out, she said with a smile, "We just experimented until we figured it out."

I replied, "Did you find that solution online somewhere?" Nope. They just figured it out on their own. Bingo! They were filled with such an abundance of joy and confidence telling me about how they struggled and figured things out on their own. It was a moment that made me feel like celebrating.

As you journey into this adventure, bringing Making to your school or classroom, you will hear stories like this from your kids. Allow yourself time to stop and "smell the roses" because if you are anything like me, these little moments will fuel you like nothing else can.

MY NOTES

DAY 70-71

TOPIC/ACTIVITY:

Team building and informal evaluation tool

OBJECTIVE(S):

1. Students continue to develop resilience and teamwork

2. Teachers facilitate an activity which allows deeper understanding of individual students and group dynamics

Coach's Notes:

This activity is more for you than it is for your students. As they work and you are able to step back and look closely at how they are working, it will give you more insight into the strengths and challenges of your class.

FURTHER EXPLANATION:

In a paper lunch sack or other container, place a small handful of mini marshmallows and a small handful of regular toothpicks. (They don't need to be counted, but try to get around 15 marshmallows and 10-15 toothpicks)

Have students get into teams of two (make sure each team has some big paper to write and draw on and several markers of various colors)

Place the sack in front of them.

Say NOTHING and wait a minute or two.

Quietly walk around the class... Observe what they do.

When someone finally asks what the bag is for, say "it's for you to decide, I'm not giving you any instructions."

Give them 10 minutes or so to tinker with the materials.

Do: Quietly walk the class and observe student behavior.

Make note of who is drawn to working together and who is more of an independent learner.

Let them find their own path. Don't coerce them to build anything specific and don't force them to work together on a single thing. During this process, the teacher is completely silent, allowing you to really see your kids and understand what makes them tick.

Once the time is up, ask them to describe what they built. It can be done using drawings, lists, paragraphs, etc. (2-3 minutes)

Make note of their communication style; is it bulleted lists, pictures, etc?

Discuss: Ask them to describe how their partner influenced what they built. (a couple of minutes)

Conclude with a discussion about values for your class.

Say: Now that we've had some time to explore and get to know one another, let's begin exploring what we collectively value in this class - what's important to us?

Student voice only here. Allow the class to brainstorm and communicate what's important to them.

Put the various suggestions up on the board and then let them use a marker to place a star next to the three-to-five they feel are the most important.

Perhaps one of your students will want to design a poster that can be printed and hung to showcase the values of the class.

Use whatever time is left of this two day activity to write, update websites, etc.

Discuss: Take about 3-5 minutes at the end of class for students to discuss, share and reflect as a group.

MATERIALS AND RESOURCES USED:

- Paper lunch bags

- Mini marshmallows

- Small toothpicks

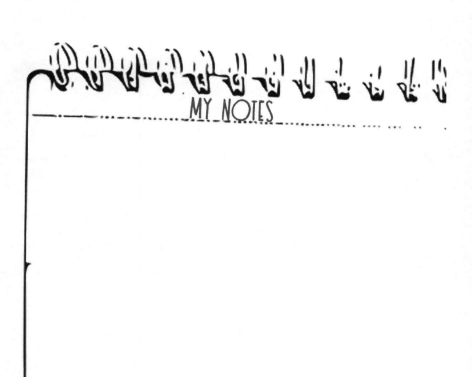

MY NOTES

DAY 72-73

TOPIC/ACTIVITY:

Brain break (you can do this, or something else of your choosing)

OBJECTIVE(S):

1. Students build resilience through the process of working hard followed by a period of mental rest

Coach's Notes:

Similar to the last brain break. There was a point in the year where we discovered the more difficult challenges and activities required more frequent brain breaks. Watch your class and be on the lookout for mental fatigue. When we started seeing that, we implemented brain breaks on most Fridays, which fit well with the increase in depth and complexity of the activities and contributed wonderfully to student success.

FURTHER EXPLANATION:

Pick a team building challenge of your choosing, either from the following list, or something else you feel will best suit your class.

Dr. Gerstein's blog User Generated Education once again served as an invaluable resource to us here. Her post titled, "Team Building Activities That Support Maker Education, STEM, and STEAM" was full of great ideas that we used throughout the year.

Team Building Activities:

- Search Pinterest for "Engineering challenges with Keva Planks"

- Marshmallow challenge

- Straw bridge building

- Dr. Gerstein's list: http://bit.ly/2aK2BO3

- Bridge building hyperdoc (compliments of Noelle and Teachers Give Teachers): http://ow.ly/krkc302rVlN

- Mystery build challenges (compliments of Noelle) http://bit.ly/29ZW9B3 | http://bit.ly/2auF7KF | http://bit.ly/2ahk1yK

Discuss: Take about 3-5 minutes at the end of class for students to discuss, share and reflect as a group.

MATERIALS AND RESOURCES USED:

- Maker notebooks

- Materials required for your chosen team building activity

REFLECTIONS:

Every time we offered one of these brain breaks and team building activities, we would talk afterward and there was complete agreement that they were a necessary part of the rhythm of the class.

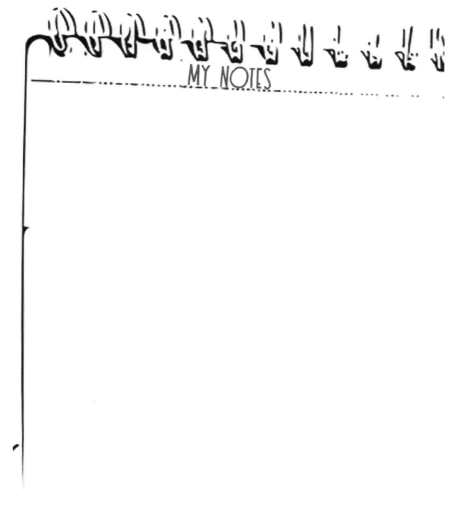

MY NOTES

Makerspace Mid Year Check In

Form description

Period 3 or period 5? *

○ Period 3

○ Period 5

This class is exciting to me *

	1	2	3	4	5	
Meh. Not that great.	○	○	○	○	○	SUPER exciting!

I get extra help when I need it in this class *

○ Yes

○ No

I feel like I have the tools I need to learn and have fun in this class *

○ Yes

○ No

I feel like I am gaining knowledge of things I never knew about before in this class *

○ Yes

○ No

If I had the chance to take this class again next year, I would consider enrolling *

	1	2	3	4	5	
Probably not	○	○	○	○	○	Yes, I'd like to take

DAY 74

TOPIC/ACTIVITY:

Student survey

OBJECTIVE(S):

1. Students will provide feedback to teachers and coaches (if applicable) that will be used to continue program success.

Coach's Notes:

You don't know what kids are really thinking or feeling until you give them a chance to tell you anonymously, and even then, you have to really ask them to be honest, so they don't just tell you what you want to hear.

We used this survey to collect some perceptual data that was extremely helpful in ensuring we really were running a class that was cultivating the things we intended.

FURTHER EXPLANATION:

Say: We're going to take a little pause today to allow you to give us honest feedback on this class.

We created our survey using Google Forms, and students were able to then complete it on iPads, laptops or iMacs.

If you don't have access to Google Forms for this, you can use free tools such as Survey Monkey. Paper is an option if technology isn't available to you, but should be a last resort option.

Survey questions:

1. This class is exciting to me (scale of 1-5: 1=meh, not that great; 5=SUPER exciting!

2. I get extra help when I need it in this class (yes/no)

3. I feel like I have the tools I need to learn and have fun in this class (yes/no)

4. I feel like I am gaining knowledge of things I never knew about before in this class (yes/no)

5. If I had the chance to take this class again next year, I would consider enrolling (scale of 1-5: 1=probably not; 5=I definitely want to take this class again)

6. I would like to share suggestions and/or ideas for next year's class. (yes/no)

7. What are your suggestions and/or ideas for next year's class?

8. Would you like to see the hands-on element of this class used in other subjects such as English and math? (yes/no)

9. Do you have any other thoughts you'd like to share related to your makerspace class?

MATERIALS USED:

Google Forms

REFLECTIONS:

The results of our survey clearly demonstrated we were reaching and exceeding our goals in this first year.

90% of the students wanted to take the class a second time

90% felt they were gaining knowledge they didn't have before this class

88% Rated their excitement level related to the class at either a 4 or 5 on a scale of 1-5

72% Wanted to see the hands-on element of Making applied to core subjects such as English and math

In the optional feedback box, almost every student wrote something and the feedback was 100% positive. This was especially exciting for all of us, as we had a high percentage of English learners in the room and seeing them want to write was an accomplishment in itself!

MY NOTES

DAY 75-76

TOPIC/ACTIVITY:

Rocket engineering

OBJECTIVE(S):

1.   Students will learn and use the engineering design process

Coach's Notes:

Having just completed two fairly large and complex projects, we wanted to do something that was a bit shorter in duration and allowed the students to engage in a more active activity that would get them outdoors for a couple of days.

The outdoor piece came directly from student requests to spend some time working outside the walls of the classroom.

FURTHER EXPLANATION:

We had launchers donated by a friend who used them at the Maker Showcase at the fair, so we didn't have to fabricate those.

There are a ton of great instructables and other plans for various (and inexpensive) DIY stomp rocket launchers out there. To save you time searching, here's one example: http://bit.ly/2aK3NkD

Rocket instructions:

1. Have students decorate their card stock while it's still flat (this makes it much easier than doing it once it's been rolled up)

2. Take one piece of card stock and wrap it longways around the pipe (We cut a couple of separate pieces of pipe to do this so students weren't all crowding around the launcher to make their rocket body)

3. Tape in 3 places along the pipe - this creates the body of your rocket

4. Cut out fins (3 or 4), fold along dotted line and tape to rocket body (We encouraged students to try different numbers of fins to see how that affected their launch. If they wanted to use only one, I said "Ok, let's see how that works.")

5. Put finished rocket onto launcher pipe for stability

6. Tape nose end shut (to seal air leaks)

7. Place cotton ball inside rocket (to keep the tape from sticking to the end of the launch pipe)

Once all of your students have finished their rockets, it's launch time!

Everyone say: "clear launchpad!"

Initialize countdown … 3...2...1… LAUNCH!

STOMP!

Do: Have students keep track of their rocket's data in their Maker notebooks, such as distance from launcher to landing, sketching estimated trajectory, etc.

Time permitting, you can allow them to re-launch to see if they can beat their last launch numbers.

BUILT IN OPTIONS:

If students want to photograph or video the launches, that would be wonderful. You'll want to continue reinforcing the "documentarian" piece that generates collaboration and support between your Makers and your broader community.

Discuss: Take about 3-5 minutes at the end of class for students to discuss, share and reflect as a group.

MATERIALS AND RESOURCES USED:

- Rocket launcher (PVC pipe, glue, old bike inner tube, pipe clamp)

- 8.5x11 card stock for rocket body

- Rocket fin templates on card stock

- Tape

- Large cotton balls

- Markers and other materials for decorating

• Empty 2 liter soda bottles (rinsed out)

REFLECTIONS:

This activity really came to life when our students were able to reflect on their experiences of the first create/launch cycle and use that knowledge to tweak their design and try again for better results.

> *It's important to note that the Maker philosophy is about exhibition, not competition. We were very careful to stay away from students competing against one another in this exercise and instead encouraged them to focus on beating their own launch data on their second try. No prizes need to be given as the true reward comes in the sense of pride and accomplishment students feel when they are allowed to create and learn in this way.*

MY NOTES

DAY 77-89

TOPIC/ACTIVITY:

Marble run stories

OBJECTIVE(S):

1. Students continue honing engineering and design skills while also building on their ability to write down their ideas

Coach's Notes:

This activity ran up to the last day of school before Thanksgiving break. You'll want to plan for that in your own scheduling, so you don't have students starting something before and then trying to pick it up after the break.

FURTHER EXPLANATION:

Printable lesson (compliments of my teacher friend Dana Brent): http://bit.ly/2ar5ik2

My Marble Run Story:

Students will:

1. Choose a story for their marble run (example, use the story of Little Red Riding Hood to create your run (i.e. avoiding the big bad wolf, etc)

2. Write their story and draw pictures inside their shoe box lid to depict the pieces of their story.

3. Sketch the outline of the marble run, complete with story elements

4. List materials required to complete

5. List anticipated costs (Dana used this as a way to open discussion about producing products and incorporate some math concepts into the activity):

_____ Box   x $5.00   = $_____

_____ Sticks   x $1.00   = $_____

_____ Notched Sticks   x $2.00   = $_____

_____ Golf Tees   x $4.00   = $_____

_____ Marbles   x $3.00   = $_____

_____ Cups of glue   x $1.00   = $_____

_____ 24" Tape   x $1.00   = $_____

_____ Paperclips (2)   x $1.00   = $_____

Cost of cutting sticks _____ min   x $1.00   = $_____

Cost of building   _____ min   x $1.00   = $_____

Total Anticipated Costs= $_____

Actual Costs

Size of box   _____

Equipment cost

_____ Box   x $5.00   = $_____

_____ Sticks   x $1.00   = $_____

_____ Notched Sticks   x $2.00   = $_____

_____ Golf Tees   x $4.00   = $_____

_____ Marbles   x $3.00   = $_____

_____ Cups of glue   x $1.00   = $_____

_____ 24" Tape   x $1.00   = $_____

_____ Paperclips (2)   x $1.00   = $_____

Total cost of building $_____

Once students have completed their projects, they will use the following questions to reflect on their process:

How close was your initial sketch to your final project?

How close were your anticipated costs to your total cost of building?

If you were to repeat this project, what would you do differently?

Once students were done with the process above, we had them once again present their work to the class, with one additional option:

They were allowed to create a video presentation to show to the class OR they could present in person.

Discuss: Take about 3-5 minutes at the end of class for students to discuss, share and reflect as a group.

MATERIALS AND RESOURCES USED:

- Shoe box lids (A local chain shoe store donated lids to us and could have them ready to pick up as long as we gave them enough notice of needing them)

- Popsicle sticks

- Small marbles or round beads for use in the run

- Glue

- Markers

REFLECTIONS:

It was great to see what they did with the video presentations! It was also fun to hear the fantastic stories they concocted for their marble runs. Being able to see our kids use their imagination in new ways and then seeing them apply those newfound skills to other projects was very gratifying.

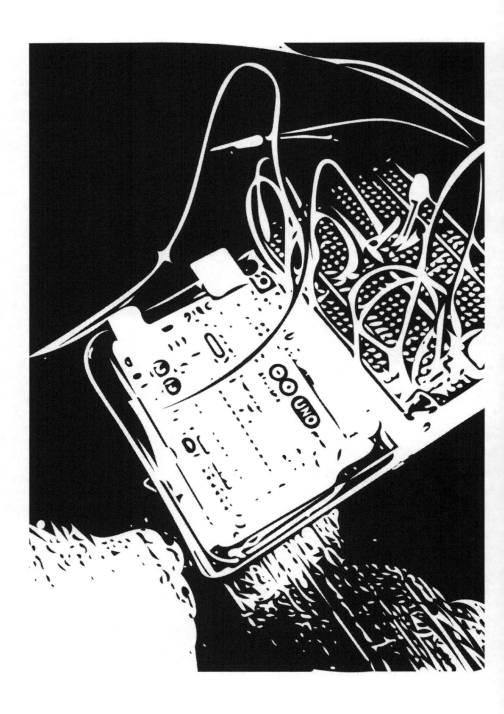

MY NOTES

DAY 90-95

TOPIC/ACTIVITY:

Hour of Code activities - times 6!

OBJECTIVE(S):

1. Students get a general understanding of computer code, the basic concepts and how code relates to the world around them.

Coach's Notes:

In teaching code, you are not just teaching skills related to computer science. Coding is a great way to build logical thinking and problem solving skills, as well as a host of other skills that will contribute to your students' abilities to persevere through challenges in a variety of situations not related to technology.

FURTHER EXPLANATION:

Noelle provided some great resources for this section, which can be found here: http://bit.ly/2ahWsqo.

Do: Introduce the concept of coding on the first day using a short, engaging video followed by a few minutes of open ended, student led discussion. On subsequent days, open each class with a new video and

2-3 minutes of student discussion.

Coding is a topic that can be terrifying to both teachers and students, so starting it off with some common language overview and explanation is very helpful to alleviate the normal fear. The website code.org has a collection of great videos for this purpose, which you can find here: https://code.org/educate/resources/videos.

Students will spend the alloted time this week exploring their choice of the activities listed in the Google Doc Noelle provided.

Coach's Notes:

Choose videos that are short - like under five minutes. They are meant to be moments that generate some "wow factor" and big thinking prompting students to be curious and to ask questions. They are not meant to "teach" your students code.

Discuss: Take about 3-5 minutes at the end of class for students to discuss, share and reflect as a group. This time is especially valuable as the sharing will help keep the exploration lively and engaging for the whole class.

MATERIALS AND RESOURCES USED:

* http://bit.ly/2ahWsqo

* code.org

* Laptops

REFLECTIONS:

I took several programming classes in college as part of my major and I distinctly remember the very first class that was required: Introduction to computer science. It was all programming in a language called QBasic, taught by an amazing female professor.

For me, with absolutely no experience with code prior to that class, it felt like we started out somewhere in the middle, not at the beginning, as we do here in these activities.

It was a serious challenge for me to learn the lingo, along with the concepts and the syntax of my first programming language, but I did it. Luckily, this professor was patient and available to her students, and she helped me understand the fundamental elements I was missing which allowed me to be successful in her class.

I did well enough that the college hired me as a part time tutor for struggling students. They gave me a classroom and supplies and I began holding regular sessions after class to go over the assignments and support others in their learning. It was great fun!

The biggest thing I came to realize about computer programming was that being able to write code provided a wonderful sense of empowerment. I now had the ability to create something from nothing that actually did stuff. Cool stuff! Having the power to control a computer - something that is to most people, a black box of mystery - brings a sense of empowerment that you can't find anywhere else.

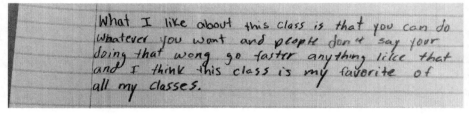

What I like about this class is that you can do whatever you want and people don't say your doing that wong go faster anything like that and I think this class is my favorite of all my classes.

MY NOTES

DAY 96-106

TOPIC/ACTIVITY:

Coding with tangible devices: Digital Sandbox and Arduino.

OBJECTIVE(S):

1. Students will apply their understanding of the basics of coding and debugging to tangible objects and sensors.

2. Students will develop skills and strategies for problem solving and iterative design.

Coach's Notes:

Remember to break up this activity with brain breaks and/or team building activities as needed. We also recognized the good that came from going outside to do these things when the weather allowed. The survey and feedback from the kids identified their desire to be outside was a high priority and the time spent outside the walls of the classroom was well worth it. Nature, sunlight, and fresh air will do wonders for your class!

FURTHER EXPLANATION:

This activity is broken up into two sections: the Digital Sandbox and

Arduino. Students will spend a few days working first with the Sandbox and then will move on to the Arduino (optional).

Digital Sandbox Activity:

This activity introduces coding in a tangible way through the use of the interactive circuit board, the Digital Sandbox. This activity is a good next step for students who have already learned coding basics through tools such as code.org as well as an easy entry point for any level, from novice to advanced users.

STEP 1:

Show provocation video to kick off activity: https://youtu.be/6C8O-JsHfmpI

Debrief video, asking students what they wonder about or are curious about after seeing the video.

Now show behind the scenes video: https://youtu.be/7YqUocVcyrE, giving students an opportunity to have some of their questions answered, and possibly prompt new things to be curious about.

Quick debrief of video, asking a couple more probing questions of your students.

STEP 2:

Give students a brief (1-2 minutes) overview of what the activity is from the "20,000 foot level" and have them get into groups of 2-3.

STEP 3:

Give students 5 minutes to quietly go over pages 2-3 in the Digital

Sandbox book to familiarize themselves with the various sensors and lights on the circuit board.

Share out - what did you find interesting?

Now, take 5 minutes to read the overview of the first experiment, "0: Setup, Loop and Blink"

Share out - what did you learn? What are you curious about?

STEP 4:

1. Login to your computer

2. Plug in circuit board

3. Open Arduino IDE

4. Go to tools --> Ardublock

Students are now ready to open the first experiment

Take about 10 minutes to tinker with settings, etc. - try cloning a line of code by right clicking on it or changing the # of the light you want to blink.

Share out. Sharing time at this point is critical for a successful activity. Some students will be stuck or bored and others will be alive with excitement and possibility. This share out time helps to bring the students up who are confused without the embarrassment of asking questions in front of the group.

STEP 5:

Now that all students are in a place where they can be successful and they have enough information to tinker in a more unstructured way, let them have 30-40 minutes to tinker on their own, opening experiments that are interesting to them.

Say: It's important to remember, each experiment builds on the one before it, so if you go too far ahead and feel confused, perhaps it's a good idea to go back to one of the previous experiments and then build up to the harder ones.

STEP 6:

Discuss: Final share out - ask students what they learned, what they were able to accomplish, etc.

Coach's Notes:

This entire activity can be done in one single day, or it can be broken up across multiple days. Use your judgment to identify which will work best for your kids. If you choose to go through all of these steps in the first day, you can allow students to build on their experiences on subsequent days, while still making time for the share-outs, which will support all students in having a positive experience.

Arduino Activity:

We offered this activity as an optional exploration for two reasons:

1. It's much more in-depth and the complexity level is considerably higher than that of the Digital Sandbox. Students really have to be interested in coding and electronics to have the desire to dive deeper into these topics, and honestly, it's really ok if they're not

interested. That's what making is all about; figuring out what is personally interesting and exciting and diving into those things.

2. To continue encouraging students to feel empowered through choice and exploration. If we never offer them choices, they will never know what to do in life when no one is there to make decisions for them. Again, it's not about us assigning kids projects because those topics are important to us, it's about kids deciding what's important to them personally and having encouraging and supportive adults there to mentor them along their journey.

STEP 1:

We produced a mini-documentary of a project we created using an Arduino which incorporates breadboarding, coding, linkages, a servo and some fun engineering and crafting. Show this or a similar video to give your kids some insight into what they can do with these tools: https://youtu.be/28vXzCsVgbs

STEP 2:

Use this site (http://stemify.weebly.com/arduino.html) to walk through some scaffolded activities structured to help kids (and teachers) understand how the breadboard and Arduino work together and how to write code to make it do interesting things.

Do: Encourage students to explore Instructables following these exercises to find more activities to try with their tools.

Coach's Notes:

You can go a long way with this, if the motivation is there and for some of your students, they will find that these activities give them a sense of empowerment they don't get anywhere else. This is their

time to take that and run with it.

MATERIALS AND RESOURCES USED:

- Digital Sandbox

- Laptops with software installed

- Arduino kits

REFLECTIONS:

I have been working with kids and coding for several years now and have found that the beginning of these activities is interesting and exciting for just about every kid. Beyond that initial point, coding is hard. It's sometimes frustrating.

For those who really enjoy it, the difficult and frustrating experiences set the stage for massive wins when you get past them. Having some personal experience with that, I can tell you there isn't really anything in the world that comes close to this feeling. Coding will resonate with some kids in a profound way and we must offer those kids an open road to cultivate their coding skills. For everyone else, when coding gets tough, they lose interest, and that's ok. Allow them to have the experience and to stay in the place that makes it exciting. There's a vast world of cool things out there and coding is just a tiny piece of it.

MY NOTES

DAY 107-121

TOPIC/ACTIVITY:

Engineering Challenge

OBJECTIVE(S):

1. Students will further develop their understanding of engineering principles, iterative design and the connections engineering has to the world around them.

Coach's Notes:

We ran this activity in connection with an actual engineering challenge, called "#EngineerThat," offered by the amazing folks at KQED, the public media station for Northern California. They put together a wonderful set of web pages, videos and additional tips, which can be found here: http://ww2.kqed.org/quest/2015/10/16/ engineerthat/. I would encourage you and your students to explore these pages, videos and resources as you roll out this activity.

The engineering challenge is built upon KQED's notes and framework, included here with their permission.

FURTHER EXPLANATION:

Do: Continue to build documentation and sharing skills by having students take photos, short video clips and jot down notes for use later on.

Before you begin, read the following information on the challenge (compliments of KQED Science):

> "The world is full of interesting problems to solve.
>
> We are all constantly observing and assessing what's not working around us, and thinking of ways to improve it. That is the heart of engineering: being curious about a problem, investigating potential solutions, and designing and testing those solutions.
>
> **The Challenge:**
>
> Identify a problem at school, at home, or in your community that can be solved or improved through engineering. You may have an idea already. Is there a water fountain that could be designed to waste less water? Could you redesign lighting at school to be more energy efficient? What's your vision for how to redesign something to make it better? We encourage you to interview friends, family members and leaders in your neighborhood to gather ideas.
>
> Define the criteria and constraints. What are the characteristics your design needs in order to be successful?

Take into account relevant scientific principles, and impacts on people and the environment. What are the limitations of your design? Think about the materials you'd need, the physical size of your product, cost, etc.

Come up with a possible solution based on your criteria and constraints. You are not required to actually build your solution, just to develop the idea and visually explain it. You can sketch your idea on paper or in a drawing app, build a prototype using everyday materials, or show your design in another way. You may want to gather feedback on your original solution and make changes to your design.

Create a piece of media that clearly explains the problem and why it needs to be solved, describes the constraints and shows your solution. Options for this could be short videos (no more than 2 mins), photos, drawings, images or infographics."

Optional idea: Share at your school or with your community - this could be a really great opportunity to engage others in your students' work in the makerspace. Students could present their innovative ideas in a demo or mini science fair format. As always, make it real for them. Something beyond just an assignment. Tie it to the real-world and real people outside your classroom as much as possible. If you're lucky enough to have a community-minded engineering firm or two in your area, explore ways to engage them in this project.

Discuss: Take about 3-5 minutes at the end of each class for students to discuss, share and reflect as a group.

MATERIALS AND RESOURCES USED:

Materials used will depend entirely on what students choose to create.

REFLECTIONS:

Our kids had a tough time with everything that involved engineering. I wonder how much of it had to do with the fact that, for most of them, this was their very first introduction to this topic. Couple that with high poverty, lack of exposure to engineering companies and professionals in their own community and you've got some challenges to work out.

BUT, that doesn't mean these activities weren't productive for them. The students were challenged, and some of this was difficult for them, but in the end, they learned and were engaged, which was wonderful.

Some topics, engineering being one of them, take longer to scaffold, depending on your students. If your kids come from demographics like ours, this is an important thing to recognize. It will be tough at times, but it is so worth it in the end.

From Noelle:

"With the engineering challenge I think that it is really important that kids talk to people in the community. Get ideas and other viewpoints. Looking back, this is something I wish we had been able to do for this activity. I would really stress the importance of that.

Also, I would have the kids do a pitch to people in the

community or school. They need to really revise and get input from the outside for this activity."

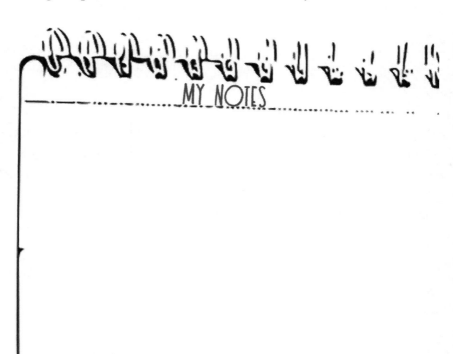

MY NOTES

DAY 122

TOPIC/ACTIVITY:

Brain break (you can do this, or something else of your choosing)

OBJECTIVE(S):

1. Students build resilience through the process of working hard followed by a period of mental rest

Coach's Notes:

Similar to the last brain break. There was a point in the year where we discovered that the more difficult challenges and activities required more frequent brain breaks. Watch your class and be on the lookout for mental fatigue. When we started seeing that, we implemented brain breaks on most Fridays, which fit well with the increase in depth and complexity of the activities and contributed wonderfully to student success.

FURTHER EXPLANATION:

Pick a team building challenge of your choosing, either from the following list, or something else you feel will best suit your class.

Dr. Gerstein's blog User Generated Education once again served as an invaluable resource to us here. Her post titled, "Team Building Activities That Support Maker Education, STEM, and STEAM" was full of great ideas that we used throughout the year.

Team Building Activities:

- Search Pinterest for "Engineering challenges with Keva Planks"

- Marshmallow challenge

- Straw bridge building

- Dr. Gerstein's list: http://bit.ly/2aK4HgR

- Additional resources compliments of Noelle: Bridge building hyperdoc http://ow.ly/krkc302rVlN, Mystery Build Cost Sheet: http://ow.ly/9BZN302rVCa

Discuss: Take about 3-5 minutes at the end of class for students to discuss, share and reflect as a group.

MATERIALS AND RESOURCES USED:

Dependent upon activity chosen for brain break.

MY NOTES

DAY 123-133

TOPIC/ACTIVITY:

LEGO Robotics obstacle course

OBJECTIVE(S):

1. Students apply their knowledge of coding and engineering in a deeper, more tangible way.

Coach's Notes:

This activity offers a return to coding with a fun challenge: build a robot and program it to run an obstacle course created by students.

As a fun side-note, the illustration of the robot featured on the preceding page is actually one my husband and I welded out of old, unused parts from my Studebaker Lark. His name is Preston Robot III. We use him to introduce coding. He's got a built in circuit with two pieces: one runs his eyes, which can be programmed to be lit dimly or brightly and his little red LED heart, which I usually start by programming to blink like a beating heart.

I let classrooms borrow Preston on long term loan, where the kids get to change up the existing code, making his heart and eyes do whatever they want. It's a fun and simple introduction to the more complex stuff you can get into with the LEGO Mindstorms or Parallax devices.

FURTHER EXPLANATION:

Do: Have your students form teams and instruct each team to build a robot.

Allow for choice in building and design, while having them keep in mind that their objective is to traverse an obstacle course.

Weather permitting, when you're ready to have robots run the course, place two parallel lines of masking tape on the ground outside, incorporating sharp turns, u-turns, sweeping curves etc.

Then students will program their robots to run the course. The robots will need to navigate the course without touching the boundaries of the tape.

Nominate a time-keeper and document each robot's time needed to complete the course. Give students an opportunity to modify their code and run the course several times to try and beat their last score.

Students' Maker notebooks will come in handy as they note their program settings and adjustments to achieve the best time for their robot.

> *It's important to have students compete with their own times, not with each other. We don't want to have a "winner" and a "loser" at the end of this activity.*

Complete the activity with entries on each student's website to describe their experience, share pictures, videos, etc. that will be shared with the class through either formal or informal presentations.

Discuss: Take about 3-5 minutes at the end of class for students to discuss, share and reflect as a group.

MATERIALS AND RESOURCES USED:

- LEGO robots or other similar devices

- Masking tape

REFLECTIONS:

Phil's reflections:

> "I had student volunteers lay down the masking tape for the course. I gave them some guidelines and then had them sketch their plan on the board, offering a little guidance before approving it.
>
> I also had them put the course inside the classroom. There was plenty of room and it made it easier to test their robot and then get right back on the computer to tweak it, plus I didn't have to worry about the very excitable noise that would be outside by other classrooms.
>
> The whole process from building the robots to running the course took longer than expected. We didn't worry about a time keeper. Nobody finished the course, but the excitement grew with each group, every time their robot went further."

The last part of what Phil offers here is especially important! Remember it's not about the product or the end goal. Ever. It's about the journey, and every student's journey will be different.

MY NOTES

DAY 134-152

TOPIC/ACTIVITY:

Cardboard engineering design challenge

OBJECTIVE(S):

1. Students become familiar with creating and working with simple machines and simple materials (cardboard, paperclips, pencils, etc)

Coach's Notes:

The following two videos are examples of what our students created for this activity. They are fantastic examples of the fabulous things you can make with cardboard and the overwhelming sense of joy you'll get to see on your students' faces when they get their design to work.

https://youtu.be/egSc.JXlj8bI

https://youtu.be/GJA-u7rozcs

FURTHER EXPLANATION:

Research resources: Pinterest, Instructables, YouTube (search cardboard engineering, cardboard automaton, cardboard machines

Do: Allow students the choice to work in groups or independently on this activity.

This activity entails designing and building a cardboard contraption that incorporates at least two simple machines AND is powered by an arduino circuit board and motor or servo.

Discuss: Students will likely need some time to discuss and learn what a simple machine is and how it works. A quick web search will return a plethora of resources to begin this discussion, including YouTube videos of working models that can be used as a provocation tool.

Students will spend a few days researching designs and ideas. Once each student or group has decided on a design, they will sketch the design in their Maker notebooks.

Once a design has been approved by the teacher, they are free to use available materials to create their contraption.

Do: Let your students know it is perfectly normal to take several tries before they are able to get a working machine.

Complete the activity with entries on each student's website to describe their experience, share pictures, videos, etc. and informal sharing of posts with class/teacher

Presenting

Students will spend this week finishing their web entries, preparing presentations, presenting on the last two days.

Discuss: Take about 3-5 minutes at the end of class for students to discuss, share and reflect as a group.

MATERIALS AND RESOURCES USED:

- Cardboard

- Paperclips

- Pencils

- Arduino kit

REFLECTIONS:

Phil's reflections:

> "For some reason I had to continually remind my students to make sure they had at least 2 simple machines and to be able to tell me where they are and what they are.
>
> They were not getting it. It was kind of like they were being lazy and not researching. But - this was a great fail and fix project.
>
> Students would test their designs and something wouldn't work the way they wanted it to, they would work together to fix it. Several times mind you. I loved this project as a teacher. No group decided to use the Arduinos but they ended up with some pretty great designs in the end. One group created a working hand, which was pretty cool."

I appreciate Phil adding his notes here. It lets us in to the reality of these classes and these plans and reminds us once again, they are a guide to be used as you see fit.

Phil's students struggled with engineering the cardboard portion of this activity and asking them to add the arduino piece would have set them up for too much expectation and not enough experience to get there.

Additionally, his comment about the kids getting a little lazy could mean a couple of things: it could mean the kids need a brain break or it could mean they need to have the activity tweaked a little to make it more meaningful and relevant to them. Engage them in this conversation and decision process.

> *Empower your students to help you find the best "fit" for them and they will reward you with their attention and their enthusiasm every time.*

Everyone's kids are going to be different, so change these activities up and make them work for your kids. If they are engaged and need more time, give it to them. If they finish earlier, great! Your implementation of this plan is what will ultimately make it work in amazing ways.

MY NOTES

DAY 153-157

TOPIC/ACTIVITY:

Free Choice Week (AKA building resilience, so kids can dive into the next big project, wink, wink!)

OBJECTIVE(S):

1. Students engage in guided exploration which builds on everything they've learned so far and offers an opportunity to dive deeper into an area of interest.

Coach's Notes:

The Harvard Business Review article reference earlier in the book says it all. Students need to have opportunities to build resilience. They also need opportunities to build the capacity to make choices, be responsible and explore in ways that allow them to discover personal interests. This type of activity is critical in establishing those building blocks that will help them achieve lifelong success.

FURTHER EXPLANATION:

This is what I wrote to the teachers I supported in the Adventures in Making class:

"Let's give students some options of things to work on and allow them some free explore time and time for creative play. This would be a wonderful opportunity to do some art projects, learn more about the Adobe apps or dive a little deeper into coding and robotics for those who are interested."

Coach's Notes:

For kids who need a little help with ideas: we found some great inspiration on Pinterest, including documentary videos of previous projects, art fingerprints, and illustrated stories and comics. Searching any of these keywords will provide an endless sea of inspiration.

Discuss: Take about 3-5 minutes at the end of class for students to discuss, share and reflect as a group.

REFLECTIONS:

Phil's reflections:

"This activity gave my students the opportunity to revisit old projects and try to make them better or go and explore something new. This was a definite must and kids enjoyed it."

What more can I say? When I read Phil's comments for this section, I smiled and thought to myself, "Yay, we did the right thing here!"

I've had conversations with some (not all, mind you) administrators during activities like this one where I get that sideways eye look from them when I say we're letting the kids decide on their own what to work on for a few days. I even had one respond with, "You mean they're just playing?"

Yes, they are playing to learn and learning to play, which means they will be happier, healthier and much more successful as adults because we had the courage to give them this time when they were kids.

Don't deprive your students of moments like this, because as Phil says, it is a "definite must."

MY NOTES

DAY 158-159

TOPIC/ACTIVITY:

Reflection and documentation

OBJECTIVE(S):

1. Students will write a longer post detailing their projects, designs, and experiences in the makerspace over the course of the year.

Coach's Notes:

We specifically set time aside for this activity to happen as the focus, rather than as an add-on to the focus activity. This is an opportunity for students to spend additional time reflecting deeply on their journey and their learning as the focus.

This is where the really amazing and long-lasting light bulb moments are born.

FURTHER EXPLANATION:

Have students reflect on their experience, so far, and post something to their website, either about the project they chose to explore last week, their overall experience in the makerspace, or something they want to create in the future. Their reflections will be posted on their websites and will include photos, sketches, illustrations, videos, etc to support their writing.

MATERIALS AND RESOURCES USED:

- Student websites

- Maker notebooks

REFLECTIONS:

I can't stress enough how powerful and inspiring this year was for all of us. We got to see our kids go from being "middle schoolers" to individual people with a deeper understanding of who they were. They got to have ideas and opinions. They got to develop their skills in sharing those ideas and opinions with each other, and with us.

I will never forget the day I walked in to the class and saw groups of kids discussing things, holding their work and talking about it with each other.

> *In that moment, I thought to myself, "If Google were run by teenagers, this is what it would look like."*

It was such a powerful feeling. Knowing that the work we had done, allowed a group rural, high poverty, shy, disengaged boys and girls, to grow and become. To dream of something better and to seize the opportunity to make it so. I can't put into words how good that moment felt.

Always, always, always give yourself and your kids time to reflect. Because it's in these moments you will truly discover the profound impact that making has on everyone.

MY NOTES

DAY 160-177

TOPIC/ACTIVITY:

Rube Goldberg challenge

OBJECTIVE(S):

1. Students will use their knowledge of engineering, design and research to create their own version of a Rube Goldberg contraption.

Coach's Notes:

*This culminating activity was a lot of fun, for us and the kids! The
key is research - getting them to see what's possible and then taking
the time to figure out what they want to do with all of that inspiration
made the whole thing come to life for them.*

FURTHER EXPLANATION:

Students will research various Rube Goldberg machines and then
decide as a class what the challenge will be. This will take a bit of
planning and thought as a group.

This is the culminating event where students will have the opportunity
to apply all the things learned through the year.

Discuss: Take about 3-5 minutes at the end of class for students to discuss, share and reflect as a group.

MATERIALS USED:

Depends entirely on what your students choose to create, although you should have all of the necessary materials at this point. Anything you don't have should be inexpensive and easy to get like paper towel tubes, string, etc.

REFLECTIONS:

Phil's reflections:

"This was a fantastic culmination of all the projects and learning for the year and another great fail and fix project. Students got very creative after some research.

A bigger space would have definitely been much better. They were limited to their surroundings. My class actually ended up moving to a vacant classroom on campus so they could leave their projects up each day preserving the progress they made."

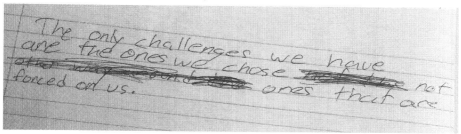

The only challenges we have are the ones we chose ... ones that are not forced on us.

MY NOTES

DAY 178-180

TOPIC/ACTIVITY:

End of year celebration and Maker showcase

OBJECTIVE(S):

1. Students will present and display their final culminating project to school, community, or other group.

FURTHER EXPLANATION:

This is time to celebrate! It's an opportunity for you and your students to reach out and speak to a wider audience about the learning and growth that took place throughout the year.

This celebration and showcase can take many forms, and will depend on availability of space, resources, and time.

Some options are a showcase at your local fairgrounds, a School Maker Faire® (school.makerfaire.com), a community showcase, or other similar event.

Making this possible will require some planning and will benefit greatly from the support of others, so be sure to allow yourself the proper time to make this happen.

The main point here is to give your students a platform for sharing their work and their experiences.

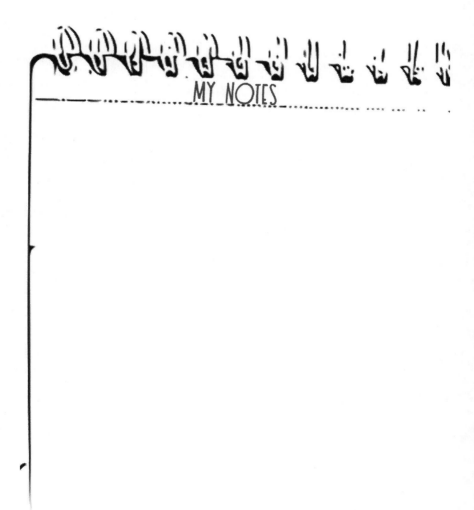

MY NOTES

Epic Advice From Noelle and Phil

I walked in the room. It was buzzing. Kids were working on different projects. Everyone was happy, engaged and definitely working. It was a beautiful thing. It was electric.

#AdobeSpark

During the summer following this class, I decided to interview Phil and Noelle for a couple of podcast episodes I was working on. They both had such amazing advice to share and some really invaluable insight into the program.

Phil's experience running the class every day and Noelle's experience working in the district as an Ed Tech support provider and regular supporter of the makerspace class are captured here. Their leadership and collaboration were pivotal in making this all work.

> *Interview transcript from Noelle McDaniel, the teacher and curriculum support provider who brought her own rare blend of rock star teacher, gritty humor and extreme dedication to this program.*

Me: Give us a little background about you and what you believe

Noelle: I have taught for 11 years from grades K-12. This past year I was the curriculum support provider for Corning Elementary School District. It was a great time to explore the exciting world of ed tech and making. I also got to watch and support our makerspace at the Middle School.

I believe that today's students are very different. They live and interact in a different world that is constantly changing. Unfortunately, I see many teachers NOT changing. This doesn't work and is not going to allow for anyone to be successful. We have changed our tests, expectations, curriculum.... But what about the delivery??

For things to be different, everything needs to be different. EVERYTHING.

Me: How does Maker education address the challenges we are facing in today's schools with preparing kids for their future?

Noelle: I really believe that students need to be learning 21st century skills. I know that is a term that gets thrown around a lot, but teachers need to focus on communication, collaboration, critical thinking and creativity. What I noticed this year in supporting a makerspace is that those four things are constantly happening. They really are the focus of every project.

> *In addition to these 21st century skills, makerspace also teaches students some other really important life skills. Things like grit, resilience, optimism, self-regulation, empathy and reflection happen everyday. These are what employers are looking for. These are the things that make people successful.*

Me: What was the biggest "aha" moment for you this year in the makerspace?

Noelle: I think the biggest "aha" moment for me was in the first weeks of makerspace. We asked the students to think of something that they were interested in for their first project. The room was silent. 90% of the kids could not tell us about a hobby, interest or something that they wanted to learn more about. It was pretty shocking.

So we had to baby step the projects. We started small, gave them choices and worked with them to a point where they could take ownership of their learning and truly create their own experiences.

I think that was my other "aha" moment. The second or third project where there were 5-10 different groups working on different things, the room was buzzing, everyone was happy, engaged and definitely working. It was a beautiful thing. I will tell people that if you are doing a great job teaching makerspace, it should be easy. You should be checking in, floating around the room, enjoying the magic.

Me: What are you excited about doing with all of this for next year?

Noelle: WOW! Where do I start? I am excited to help launch a new makerspace at DaVinci next year. I'm excited to be a makerpace teacher! I think what I want is to be someone else's "aha" moment. I want other teachers to be able to see how doing things differently WILL create an environment for our students to become successful.

I read a quote recently that said, "The point of going 1:1 is not to be paperless, it's to change the task." That really resonated with me. I am planning on going paperless next year, but I started with the idea of changing everything.

Me: What was the most important thing the district leadership has done to support your work in Maker education?

Noelle: I have been lucky to have had an administrator who understands the need for change and supports doing things differently. I think that's the biggest thing.

I have also been provided with great opportunities for trainings. I am lucky to have been able to go to some great PD.

Me: What's the most important thing you can offer to other teachers who are going into something like this?

Noelle: I think the thing that I tell teachers the most is, this didn't magically happen overnight for me. I spent a lot of time getting to where I am. It also became a passion for me. I truly believe in the makerspace and edtech movement happening in education right now.

Spend the time, get some great PD and, if you can find a great mentor or partner to work with, that is huge. If you don't have an outside consultant or a Tech Coach at your site, start your own support program. Meet and talk about what you are doing in your classroom.

SHARE! Another great quote I read (which I can't remember word for word) is "Awesome teachers share their awesome. They don't keep it contained in their rooms."

Be the change you want to see.

Me: What other support was crucial in making this happen for you and your kids?

Noelle: Amazing support from Michelle Carlson. The whole way. I was very fortunate in the fact that she was someone that my admin consulted with and listened to. She is an amazing person. (I did not coerce her to say this, hee hee!)

> *Interview transcript from Phil Mishoe, the teacher whose amazing coaching and mentoring skills brought the Adventures in Making class to life every day for his kids.*

Me: How did you feel going into this?

Phil: Right away, very nervous. Did not know what to think at all, because I've never done anything like this. I've been teaching PE for 18 years and that's what I know. So I was very anxious. I just did not know what to expect. Had a lot of questions, but also was excited, because it was something new, and it was something that had the potential to really inspire kids.

Me: What was the best part of the year for you?

Phil: Definitely seeing the kids light up when their projects would work. They would kind of go about different things, they would have some failures, and then they would fix it, rethink things, go through it again, and then just all of a sudden they're just so proud of themselves. It was great to see... For me, nothing beats that.

Me: In school, do you see opportunities for students to fail and then get back up in traditional education?

Phil: Not nearly as much as in the makerspace, not even close. A lot of the time, you turn in your homework, here's your grade, you take a test, here's your grade, and let's move on. This is completely different. You have many opportunities to correct things and become successful.

Me: How did you keep the kids motivated?

Phil: They get to decide this is what we're gonna do, we don't care what they're doing over there, we're gonna do it this way, and that just motivates them right there.

Me: How did you transition from one project to the next?

Phil: Reflection was a must, for sure. After each project, they'd do a short write or just talk to each other about what went well, what didn't go so well, what to do next time, and they'd update their Google sites... that kind of stuff.

Me: How did you come to see value in the program or see it in a different way?

> *Phil: Well, the value is tremendous for sure. Students take ownership in what they're doing. And they learn that it's okay to fail at something, knowing they're gonna have a chance to build on it, rethink things, redo things, not once, not twice, several times if they have to, until they get it right. I think the value right there is huge.*

It just drives them to want to make their project better because they know it's theirs. They approached everything thinking I'm gonna finish this, and that's gonna make it mine. I think that's a huge value for them."

Me: Did you see a big change in the kids from the beginning of the year to where you ended off the year?

Phil: Absolutely. Beginning of the year, I think they were kinda like me at the beginning of the year. They really weren't sure what to do and they weren't real motivated I think just because they maybe didn't think they had the tools and they were unsure about some of the technology we had in there. As they used it more and more and realized that they had to figure things out for themselves and try and use that technology their motivation absolutely went up. They understood.

Me: What is the most important personality trait you feel a makerspace teacher needs to have?

Phil: I think a form of free thinking, for sure. Teachers need to understand that there is more than one way to get to that end product and not every kid is going to do it the same way, not every kid thinks the same way, and so as a teacher you need to understand that as well to instill that in the kids, because that's what this class is all about. It is about those kids finding their own way to do something and be successful at it.

Me: How do you feel about knowing or not knowing all of the tech stuff going in? If you were to say "Should administrators be looking for someone who knows the technology going in or do you think it's better for someone to be going in to be a learner with the kids?

Phil: Both. That's a tough one. Me, myself, I don't know a whole lot about technology, and that was one of the scary parts of it. A lot of my students at times knew more than me about technology, which was pretty cool, really. Because as I was learning, they were teaching me. Stuff I knew, I could help them out with. So really, I think both are beneficial for sure. It would definitely help if there was a teacher that was spot on with the technology 'cause, I mean, there's a lot of it. But really, the class is about learning and figuring things out, which I've had to do right along with the kids and I think was just fine.

Me: What's the most important thing you can offer to other teachers, as advice or any other reflection, who are going into something like this?

> *Phil: Don't be afraid to just step back and watch. I remember you came in one of the classes earlier in the year and that was your advice to me: 'Step back, watch the magic happen' you know, and that was perfect, that's a huge thing to be able to do. It's kind of hard to do if you are a traditional classroom teacher because that's not what you do. To be able to step*

back and just let them go, and see what they're doing, let them be noisy, let them figure things out. It's very beneficial. So you have to be willing to do that, and you get to see them dive in and work. If you can do that, you're gonna be just fine.

Me: What support was crucial in making this happen for you and your kids?

Phil: Number one piece: Michelle Carlson and Noelle McDaniel. Absolutely. Seriously. I would have struggled so much if it wasn't for you two, one hundred percent. Your knowledge and your experience in this kind of stuff was huge for me. If I didn't have that support, if it was just me here and the rest of the staff that really didn't know much about it either, it would have been tough. I don't think the kids would have enjoyed it as much or had the successes they had this year without that support. Also, definitely, administration being willing to spend money. That has to happen. If they don't spend the money, you're not going to have those opportunities to have those successes.

If you'd like to listen to the audio version of these interviews, or share them with others, they are freely available online via here: https://soundcloud.com/user-752555821

Startup Funding & Sustainability

The following three sections are all about making sure you can get the startup and ongoing funding and support you need to change the world for your kids.

Starting a program such as this is not inexpensive, but with a little creative planning and tenacity, you *will* be able to make it happen.

Funding Your Makerspace

So, let's talk about funding. With support from leadership, funding your makerspace can be a fairly simple process, but sometimes, even with leadership support - especially in rural districts such as ours where we don't have tech industry or lots of thriving businesses in our backyard - funding can be a real challenge.

As I was writing this, I came across this absolutely perfect article by Scott Dellosso (@scott_dellosso, Maker Educator and Google Certified Educator). When I reached out to him on Twitter to ask permission to share his work, he gave a green light. This is a perfect example of the power of Twitter! I have connected with more friends and colleagues from all over the world on this platform than at all the education conferences I've attended, combined. You'll find excerpts from Scott's post on the following pages, and the full article can be found here: http://bit.ly/2bd3V8B

Admin Support

Scott talks about having support from administration, which is great, because it ties directly to our recipe for success. It is imperative that you have at least one person in your corner with the power to support your efforts. Everyone doesn't have to be on board, but you do not want to find yourself trying to bring this huge dream to life without some kind of admin support. I've seen too many teachers and friends try to run with this flag on their own and it always ends the same, no makerspace.

Scott also talks about sharing:

> It is extremely important to have the support of your su-
> periors, especially working within your school system.
> Be clear, be transparent. Tell them what you plan on
> doing. Keep them updated and in the loop. Have them

approve everything before you do it. You don't want your funds refused because you didn't follow appropriate guidelines.

Share in the excitement and the triumphs. Celebrate together and let your supporters join you in all those good moments. Be sure to also share the logistics of what you're doing. There's a certain amount of temptation to keep things a secret until the project is done. Be smart here. I've done this myself, because I knew I needed to get past the point of no return before I let *everyone* in on what I was working on. But I always, always, always kept my champion admin in the loop. Always. Honoring this relationship and this person's trust in you by entrusting them with what you're doing will ensure the trust continues.

Fundraising

Here are three options Scott shares in his post, with some really great explanation and examples. His advice is a goldmine, and in reading it for this, I gleaned some things I will employ in the future as I support the continued roll-out of these programs in my own community.

1) Traditional Fundraisers

Car washes, bake sales, and canning. While all these work just fine, this is (in my opinion) the least effective method of fundraising. There is a time factor to think about in your cost/benefit analysis. These events take enormous amounts of time to plan and execute, and unfortunately the return on funds you make for these events is not always as much as you would hope for, considering the amount of planning time that goes into each. If you are going this route, I would recommend delegation. Your time is more effectively spent in other places, but that doesn't mean you should ignore these methods. Ask parents, volunteers, or others to work one of these methods, while you focus on the two methods below (and mostly on method 3).

Yes! If you have a group of kids or parents who want to hold a car wash or a bake sale, by all means, encourage them to go forth and conquer. This is an easy way to get your community engaged in the creation of your makerspace, and allows more people to feel a sense of ownership, which is great. As for your time, however, Scott is right. There are other ways for you to raise funds that will give you a much higher return on your investment, and depending on where you are geographically, crowdfunding might just be the perfect solution. Here's some of what Scott offers for this option:

2) Crowdfunding

This method probably clocks in as the winner in terms of ease of setup and possible return on time spent. There are multiple platforms you could choose, but the idea is you set up on a site, share on social media, and watch the donations pour in from family, friends, and members of the community. One of the most popular is GoFundMe. Sign up with an email address, put in a description and some pictures, and you are ready to share! Donors easily make contributions with their credit cards and share your campaign. A few notes here:

This is GREAT for getting lots of small (10-30 dollar donations), but BAD for receiving big donations because GoFundMe holds 5% of your donation for using their service. WePay (payment processing company) holds 2.9% of your donation. It's a good idea to CLEARLY state this information in your description, and encourage those making a larger donation to do so directly to you or your organization.

Again, keep your admin in the loop and ask permission before you set up a crowdfunding campaign. As Scott states in his post, there may be rules, protocols or policies that might prevent your ability to accept funding from a campaign such as this.

Incidentally, we ran a crowdfunding campaign for this book. We didn't get funded, but we did raise over $22,000.00. We chose to use Kickstarter, which only releases funds if you meet or exceed your goal, and since we didn't meet out goal, we didn't see a penny. Not to worry, though, because you are still reading the book! Makers will always find a way to make it happen! All of the crowdfunding platforms run a little differently, which is something to consider when you're exploring your options.

My earlier note about geography matters too. Being in a rural area, most people here have never even *heard* of crowdfunding, so getting them to support us took a lot of explaining up front just to help them understand what Kickstarter is. Factor in time for this, because a successful campaign takes an intense amount of time, especially if you have to explain the technology before you even get to talk about what you're doing.

The third and final option for funding we're sharing here is probably the easiest and most fruitful; and it doesn't matter if you're rural, remote or urban, you will undoubtedly find success with this one. This option focuses on corporate and service organization sponsorships.

Scott offers some fantastic advice and examples, including who to ask, what to ask for, and how to go about it:

3) Corporate and Service Organization Sponsor-

ships Before you start, get organized. Create a spreadsheet where you can put your target audience contact information. Sending out letters and making phone calls is much easier to do all at once, and you are going to want to keep track of who you reach out to.

Leave room to note when you sent out the letter, when you did your follow-up phone call, and any notes you might want to take about the conversation you had.

Organization	Contact	Letter sent:	Phone call on:	Notes:
Town of ▓▓▓	▓▓▓ Town Hall ▓▓▓▓▓▓	letter sent 4/12/16	phone call on 4/18	mayor has meeting on may 2nd for budget, may approve beforehand
				will donate 1,000
American Legion Post ▓▓▓	▓▓▓2771 ▓▓▓2325 (office) ask for Susanne (secretary)	letter sent 4/12/16	phone call on 4/18	general meeting for approval may 4th
American Legion of ▓▓▓	Attn: Neil ▓▓ ▓▓▓9078	letter sent 4/12/16		

For most organizations, in order for their secretary or treasury department to cut a check, many will require a letter of request from you. Here are some tips for writing your letter:

Use official letterhead. It's important for these organizations to know you are legitimized. Use school letterhead, or if not at a school, use the official letterhead for your organization. If possible, use a better quality paper as well. Also, be sure to start your letter using the person's name you are writing to.

Send a picture of kids along with your letter (with

parental permission). It is important for them to see the faces of the students they will be making an impact on. You can get hundreds of standard photos printed up very inexpensively (in the area of $10-$12 for a 100).

In your first paragraph, introduce your organization and use BUZZ WORDS. Tell them exactly what students in your makerspace learn about. Use words like STEM or STEAM. When organizations hear about all the great work you are doing, especially using words they have heard in the news or on social media lately, they are more likely to get excited about being a part of it. Here is an excerpt from the first paragraph of my letter:

"In DI, students learn about 3D printing, coding, app development, drones, virtual reality, and more. It is a program that trains the future engineers, developers, inventors, and leaders of our country."

Bottom Line Up Front (BLUF). Don't bury the lead; tell them at the top of the letter you are seeking a donation. You will be writing to the CEOs, Presidents, and heads of companies. Many don't have a lot of time to dig all the way through your letter to figure out what exactly you are writing for. State it clearly: *We are seeking to raise $8,760 to support our organization moving forward.*

The BLUF principle is so important. I get quite a few requests in my inbox and being a busy person with a huge amount of responsibility running FDG, I need to know what folks are asking for right away and why they're asking. If there are good values and mission alignment, there's always time to ask for more information, a meeting or a phone chat, but that comes after you've gotten the attention of the person you're writing to.

> **Ask BIG!** Ask for way more than you are sure the organization will give you. First, arrive at a legitimate number. Do this by creating a wishlist of items you want; include how much it might cost to support those items moving forward. Use that number.
>
> Most organizations will not fully fund whatever number you put there. So if you go in asking for $500, maybe you will get $100 or $200; they know you are seeking help from multiple places, and are fine with that, but usually reluctant to fully fund any one organization asking for help. However, if you tell them you are seeking to raise upwards of $10,000, you are more likely to get something like a $1,000 donation.

After writing and being funded for quite a few small grants to support Maker programs, I can say with confidence this is very true. You will rarely get what you're asking for, so make sure you're providing the big picture, in its entirety, and asking for support in bringing your big dream to life, not just a small part of it.

Touch on the five W's in your request: who, what, where, when and why. I often use this as a checklist to make sure I haven't forgotten anything. This seems kind of silly, but it's so easy to forget an integral piece like how to get in touch with you when you're writing from your heart about a project you're very passionate about. Have several people read your letters to make sure they make sense before you send them.

> *"If you ask for the moon, you'll be surprised by how often you get it."*
> **John Green**

Once you have your letter ready to roll, send it out to as many companies and organizations as you can, and, as Scott suggests, be sure to include big corporations who are heavy users of technology, if you can. The following community organizations are generally a good place to start:

Lion's Club
Rotary Club
American Legion
VFW
Indian Casinos
Local foundations

Don't expect funding from every letter you send, so be sure and send them to as many places as you can. As Scott notes in his article, he sends about 50 letters and gets around 15 yes's, which generally provides funding anywhere from $250 to $1,000 in donations per funder.

Follow-Up and Follow-Through

This is, I think, the hardest part of the whole process. It's also the part that will get you there, so don't lose steam after you've sent your letters. Here's Scott's advice on following up and following through:

Send out your letter, writing down the day you mailed it out. Through your online research, if you can't find an address, email works fine. Scan your letter and picture, and note the day you sent out the initial email.

Follow-up phone call. It is important to speak to a human! If you sent letters USPS, wait four days to ensure they got the letter and had time to read it. Don't put this off longer than a week or two! If you wait, your letter might just end up in the circular filing cabinet. You will want to call right away.

Ask to speak to the person you sent the letter to. Asking for money can be awkward at first, but you have to just do it. After some practice, it will feel more natural. Give yourself a script if necessary. Something like:

"Hi, this is _____ from _____. We sent you a letter last week requesting a donation for _____. I was wondering if you received the letter? Are you going to be able to support us at this time?"

Take notes and follow up! Often they will have gotten the letter, but it might have to go through a committee or board first. If that's the case ask the date of meeting. Call back and follow up after.

If you can get help with this part from a parent or someone at your school, that would be great. Find as many ways as you can to empower others to help you here. If you can create your spreadsheet as a Google file that's shared, you can make this happen pretty easily.

Say Thank You

Oh my goodness, I can't tell you how important this is. I have been the recipient of a great deal of support and have also offered my time and money to support the work of others and, at both ends of the spectrum, this is essential.

To all of the organizations and people who have supported my work, I send thank you emails, photos, and have even created some videos of the kids working to share and showcase what the funding has allowed us to do. Offering support and being supported is such a human thing. So, the thank you should be human too. Here's Scott's wonderful guidance on saying thank you:

> Once you have received donations, make sure to send thank you's. You want to keep a good relationship with your donors, so when you go back in a year or two they are still happy.

> Be sure to send a thank you letter. Let the students write this one! It will be much more impactful. Ask them to talk about all the awesome things they are learning and doing.

> Give them guidance as to what to talk about, but do not edit their letter. Let there be sentence structure and grammar errors. It will be more truthful in showing the thank you is actually from the students.

> Include more pictures! Make sure to document your students using the materials and equipment you raised funds for.

> Continue to follow up throughout the year. Make offers to visit the organization to share and show all the cool stuff you are doing. Invite them to your Make-Nights or other events. Be sure to maintain contact and a good

relationship.

Running a Maker program is a long-term project and the more you can involve your community in it, the more successful you and your kids will be. Keeping them engaged will come from showing your genuine appreciation and letting them be a part of the story as it unfolds.

Thanks, Scott, for allowing us to share your advise on funding!

Sharing Student Successes

Share, share, share. This is **so** important. Not only does sharing the magic with a wider audience contribute to the "realness" of the class for your students, it also contributes to the positive buzz around your program, which will help you tremendously when seeking funding support - from inside and outside your school.

You can have the greatest thing going on earth in your classroom, but if no one knows about it, they certainly won't be thinking of how they can support you; and with a Maker program, you will definitely need ongoing support to make it work. Since this chapter is on funding and sustainability, that's the piece we are addressing here: how to share what's going on so you get the support you need to keep it alive.

One caveat before going any further: every district has a different approach to sharing student work and photos online. Make sure before you share anything, that you are aware of your district's policies and procedures and that you follow them.

Creating a Framework for Sharing:

Our framework consisted of :

- YouTube channels (teachers, students, support providers)

- Twitter

- In person communication - it's all about relationships!

- Emails to leadership and other teachers sharing specific stories of the amazing things that were happening

- And this year we're adding a class website to house links to all student sites, videos, reflections, etc.

We had several YouTube channels that housed various clips of student awesomeness and with tools like iMovie on our iPads, creating and uploading the movies was really very easy. I think the biggest hurdle that keeps teachers from using this tool is that they feel like they need to create Hollywood level video, which is sooo not necessary. I encourage you to check out my YouTube channel for examples: http://bit.ly/2bd4q2w.

The videos that will bring support to your program are the ones you can finish and publish. A couple of helpful hints for video work:

1. DO film in landscape, not portrait. I've seen videos taken by people using their phone and that tall and narrow view doesn't translate well. Watching videos like that always makes me want to lean to one side or another to see the parts that didn't get captured.

2. DO edit your videos. iMovie makes this soooo easy. Keep your overall length to under four minutes if possible. That's a filter on YouTube's search function; it's also about the maximum attention span of your viewers. If you've captured a long section of kids working, you really only need a little piece of it to make your point. Keep the content moving, engaging and focused. Again, you'll see examples of this on my channel as well as Noelle's, which is here: http://bit.ly/2bd3XgX

3. Don't make it harder than it needs to be. Simple, engaging, short and lively snapshots of kids working, interviews, and some cool

photos and you've got it made. After that, all that's left is to send your video out in an email or on Twitter with a personal note so others can join you in celebrating the great things happening in your classroom.

Speaking of Twitter, I have found more inspiration, met more amazing people and stumbled on more fantastic resources here than anywhere else. Twitter is a wonderful resource for sharing, connecting, and collaborating with people from all over the world.

There's a great article in THE Journal called 13 Great Twitter Chats Every Educator Should Check Out which will get you a strong start.

If you're new to Twitter, create an account, follow a few other educators (you can follow me @FutureDevGroup) or publications you enjoy reading and just watch for a while. Get comfortable with the dynamic of this form of communication and the system. This might take you a couple of months. Knowing that going in will help to make that initial learning experience a little less frustrating and you'll be more likely to stick with it.

Once you're feeling familiar with the tool and you've created your own community in the Twitter-verse, use it to share and connect!

Strong relationships are at the core of every successful venture. This is a key piece of the puzzle. Spend time thinking about how you will authentically cultivate these powerful networks. And, by "cultivate networks" I don't mean that weird thing that comes to mind when you hear the word "networking."

That term always kind of bothered me because it generated thoughts of stuffy, self-absorbed people looking for ways to make more money or have more power. But that's just me. (Insert rebellious smile here.)

By cultivating powerful networks and relationships, I mean, find people who care about what you're doing and care about what they're doing. It's more like building a big family than it is about having more friends. My network of passionate Makers continues to grow and I am so grateful and honored to know people who invest themselves in making the world a better place and helping others who are on that same path.

I have a dear friend and colleague who taught for several decades and, at the time of her retirement, was a highly respected lead teacher at her school. She had a favorite quote she used all the time in conversations with her team, and with me:

"Know your people."

Chances are, there will be people who support your efforts and those who don't. That's reality. Spend your time and effort honoring the ones in the former category and know that at some point, the ones in the latter will probably come around on their own.

Share with your champions. Engage them in conversation about the great things happening in your makerspace. Hopefully you will have at least one champion who has the power and authority to support you in your efforts, as this is one of the three required elements in the recipe for success.

For us, Rick was a huge champion of the work. There were many others who supported our project too, but Rick being the district superintendent, he also provided that piece of the recipe that allowed the whole thing to come to life.

Sometimes champions come from unlikely places. Get out there and connect, share your passion for the work and whatever you do, don't ever give up.

Finally, the element that ties all of this together: your class website. Creating a site is easier than you might think. Use a free tool such as Google Sites, Wix, Weebly or Wordpress.

If you're pressed for time, here's the bare bones list of things you should include on your site, which will allow you to create it and then not give it another thought:

1. Links to all of your students sites. This will keep your site fresh and current without any effort on your part as your students will be updating their sites regularly. Make this piece stand out front and center as it is the heart of your classroom's content sharing plan.

2. A link to your YouTube channel

That's it! Really. If you are regularly adding videos either you or your students have created to YouTube, and your students are following the plan and updating their sites regularly, you'll have a wonderfully vibrant and engaging class website accessible 24x7 without having to do any work beyond the initial creation. I don't know about you, but I really enjoy mixing something easy into my life every now and then.

Beyond the basics, you can also build on your website by adding:

1. A teacher blog. Noelle maintains a blog, sharing stories, thoughts, resources, etc. This additional element provides a way to connect with her work beyond the asynchronous communication of sharing videos and student work. If you have time to incorporate this piece, it will be well worth it. Here's a link to Noelle's http://bit.ly/2bd4Iq9

2. Tutorials and other resources. This could be something your students want to help you with, or something you want to take on yourself. Either way, it is at the heart of the Maker philosophy. Create, share, support. You can create tutorials on sites like Instructables and then link to them from your site, or create them within your site itself. If you do decide to create them on Instructables, you will be creating yet another avenue to tap into a Maker community which numbers in the millions.

Once you have your site up and going, we'd love to see it! Share the link on Twitter using this book's hashtag *#180DaysBook*.

Entrepreneurial Opportunities

Last but not least, there are opportunities to introduce your students to entrepreneurship in ways that can provide a regular stream of funding for the smaller supplies in your makerspace such as duct tape, LEDs, and such.

How much money this can generate depends on several factors including the size of your school, poverty index, support from admin and motivation of your students to create and sell products.

Here's how we went about doing this:

When students began the activity where they got to choose to make something for sale, we worked it out so their goods could be sold in their school's student store.

The plan was to ask them to develop a very basic business and marketing plan that included the following information:

1. Item to sell

2. Materials needed and cost to produce one item

3. How many they intended to make and at what price they wanted to sell them

4. Expected profit (selling price minus production cost)

5. How they would market their product and to what audience

6. How they would keep track of sales and profits

Our first year was a good start and we are looking forward to further developing this program in year two.

> *If in your first year, you are new to all of this, or slightly overwhelmed, my advice is to either leave this piece out entirely, or give it a try on a small scale. Whatever you do, don't try to eat the elephant all in one bite.*
>
> *This is a huge piece of the elephant that, when done successfully, can add a very exciting and worthwhile piece to your program, but it is also a lot of work and will not adversely impact anything if left out.*

Data and Evidence

> *"The intuitive mind is a sacred gift and the rational mind is a faithful servant. We have created a society that honors the servant and has forgotten the gift."*
> *- Albert Einstein*

Data is great, especially when we can see it as a piece of what's inside the toolbox, not the entire toolbox. As I said earlier in the book, we must always remember we are working with human beings, not numbers.

I'm going to be super honest with you here. This is one of those hot button topics that makes the hair stand up on the back of my neck a little, ok, maybe a lot. My rebel nature tends to reveal itself especially strong in this space.

I've seen the evidence that this works. In the faces of kids who have lost loved ones and gotten lost in the system, only to find their way again through making; and in the faces of those kids who are lost in the land of straight A's, struggling to live up to the high expectations of those around them, and finding no joy in the process. The kids who find their voice and their confidence, not in the straight A's or compliance, but in being creative and in making things that matter to them.

The evidence is intuitive for me. But not everyone can make or support decisions based on gut instinct, and I know you are going to need something more than me telling you this works to make a strong case to your admin. So, we enter this conversation carefully and thoughtfully, in order to get something constructive out of it that works *for kids*, because they must be the center of the universe when it comes to education's data driven nature.

Here are my informed thoughts on how to "prove" your Maker program is making a difference for kids:

1. First and foremost, stay away from invasive assessments and tools that make your kids feel like they are being "studied." We've got enough of those as it is. Sure, we surveyed our kids - to better understand how the class was going for them. What they enjoyed and what they didn't and what they wanted to see more of as we moved forward. This was very effective and gave students a way to voice their feelings and thoughts in safe and anonymous ways for the betterment of the program. It empowered them, let them feel important, respected and heard and they knew that their contributions would lead to positive refinements that would truly benefit them.

2. We are beginning, also, to look at data that has already been collected from students throughout the year as an additional method of showing the efficacy of our programs. Specifically, we're looking at attendance, behavior and overall academic success as indicators to use in determining program impact on enrolled students.

The fact that you're reading this book right now probably means you're in the same category as me: you get it. But, like me, you'll probably run into people who need hard numbers as you move forward. We'll be sharing our hard numbers and data on our website in the coming months at www.futuredevelopmentgroup.com. Subscribe to our blog to ensure you get notified as those things are posted.

In the meantime, EdSurge (one of my favorite online resources) recently published a fantastic article on the efficacy of maker ed, which you can find here: http://bit.ly/2akvpXK.

Making it Personal

My stories are shared here, not because I want you to know more about me; but because of the hordes of students out there who are apathetic, uninvolved, unplugged, and stuck, just like I was in school. My story is the story of kids and young adults everywhere who will find their joy, as well as their success, through Making, just as I did.

It's a story resonates with so many people, who are afraid to say what they really think or share how they really feel. When interviewing Maryn and Ericka for the podcast we mention throughout this book, both said they never felt comfortable being honest about their thoughts on school, while they were there.

It's only after graduating and moving on that they are free to say how unpleasant it was for them. They found Making in their senior year and junior years, respectively, which brought joy, growth, confidence, and understanding in very personal ways for both of them. Imagine how much better school could have been, if we'd been there for them sooner.

> *"The future belongs to the curious."*
> *Dr. Jackie Gerstein, Ed.D.*
> *Harvard Graduate School of Education*
>
> *Unfortunately, many of today's students have lost the spark of curiosity.*

Being a Maker is about more than just making things. It's also about having a fully stocked personal toolbox one can use to find solutions - to even the toughest challenges; to become curious and motivated to

201

discover the answers.

I've been a maker all my life. Growing up in a rural area, my family didn't have much. I would find myself bored, rummaging through my dad's shed for anything to use to make something fun or interesting.

I once made a night light using an old scrap of 2x4, some random copper wire I stripped of its insulation and various small automotive and household light bulbs I found. The only piece we had to buy was the battery that made it work. My night light had a switch and gave off a lovely glow when lit. I think I was about ten years old when I made that and I made many more contraptions over the years to occupy my time.

Over the next couple of decades, I grew up, figured out how to fund a college education and got married - all pretty normal stuff. In the early 2000's, my husband, Jim, and I decided that we wanted to own our own home, but in the height of the housing market, it was out of our reach - or was it? He's a maker too.

We realized that with Jim's construction skills, we could build our own home, and so we did.

Almost 10 years later, I had a crazy idea to restore a classic car, which was born out of my dad's "when I was a kid" stories from life in the 50's and 60's, and all the super cool cars he bought "for a song" and fixed up. His stories were about making something his own, something that became a part of who he was.

My dad and I often talked about how fun it would be to restore an old car together. It was just a dream, until one day, I said, "Why not?" I could buy the car cheap and, if we did all the work ourselves, it could be done at a fraction of the cost most people pay for restorations.

I went to work trying to convince Jim this was a good idea. His first argument against it was, "We don't know anything about restoring classic cars, how do you expect we'll even know what to do?"

My response: "You can learn anything on the Internet!"

He had no argument that would stand up to that. Because you can literally learn anything on the Internet.

> *I'm not sure the rest of the education world has totally caught up to this concept yet, and this is another place where Maker education has the power to usher in some pretty profound change. It's about putting the tools in the hands of kids and empowering the kids themselves to use them.*

Jim eventually gave into my insane idea...making my lifelong dream a reality. We purchased this 1960 Studebaker Lark hardtop, and when the pile of rusty metal got delivered to Jim's shop, everyone thought I was crazy.

As the months went by and the car began to look like a car again, the quizzical looks I had been getting early on changed to admiration.

A year later, we had this (pictured with my two real-life heroes, left: Jim (aka hubby) and right: dad (aka pops):

My burning desire to make things, to bring dreams to life (both my own and the kids that I work with everyday), coupled with my slightly rebellious attitude helped me reach a place today where I am certain I can do anything. Isn't this the kind of empowerment we want for all our children? These skills also gave me the confidence I needed to create my own job, in a place where good jobs are not plentiful.

Not only do I get to spend 100% of my time inspiring and supporting others in this work, I get to use my story as an example, letting kids and adults alike see that pursuing your dreams is something you should never be discouraged from doing. Being a Maker makes the world a better, more joyful place for everyone.

As Maryn said earlier in the book, "Isn't that what education is about? A child with such a burning desire to learn something that when given the raw materials and resources they use their love to pursue the knowledge themselves."

I would add one more thought to Maryn's statement: School can be a place where young people can build themselves and in turn, build their own future; one that is personal, unique, and fulfilling.

With Maker Education at it's core, education can be transformed from what it is to what it can be.

> *"In the 50's and 60's, Making was about knowing how to fix your car and how to make a better home, and a lot of other stuff. Not just those things though...It was about making your life better."*
> **Dale Dougherty**
> **Founder & CEO, Maker Media, Inc.**

School was not that place for me, and is not that place for far too many disinterested, apathetic students today. I didn't learn any of the things that allowed me to build my own home, or restore my own car, or create my own dream job in school. I learned from my parents, and my mentors and my sometimes very challenging life experiences. Unfortunately, not every kid has the opportunity to learn or be supported in this way, which makes their time in school even more critical to their success in life.

What I experienced in school is the reason I am so passionate about bringing this change to our kids and our country.

I see our system is one of compliance. The system asks administrators to comply. Administrators ask teachers to comply. Teachers ask students to comply. The whole thing is based on the premise that *I tell you to do something and you do it.*

The result is millions of kids who's greatest skill is to wait to be told what to do and then do it. Some kids can go along with this just fine. They are happy to do what they are told. They are the "good students" - eager to live up to the expectation, do what is asked of them to get that warm and fuzzy feeling when they see the A or B at the top of their work. But what happens when they transition into adulthood and no one is there to provide that structure anymore? Options and choices paralyze, instead of providing possibility and wide-open promise.

In an online interview with Maryn and Ericka, two teens from very different backgrounds and abilities, they shared their stories of spending 18 years of their lives creating themselves to try and live up to what the system expected, only to find, that at the end of all of it, they didn't have any idea who *they* were.

Ericka shares a story about her first job interview, where she was asked the question, "What are you good at?" and she had no idea how to answer.

Upon discovering the makerspace, Maryn and Ericka discovered themselves. They've both discovered their interests, and their ability to give themselves the grace and diversity they need in life to feel good about who they are and where they're headed. You can listen to their very profound talk here: http://bit.ly/2aR15tH

Their stories resonated with me and brought back memories of my own experiences, being asked to create myself around someone else's image of who I was. There were many teachers over the years who gave me *"the talk:"*

> *"You are so smart...you have so much potential...you need to see that...you need to do this...you should be doing that."*

All these talks did for me was further extend the chasm between me and "my potential."

Today, school still asks for compliance in many places. But the world asks for something entirely different. It asks for young adults who can be aware of their surroundings, identify problems that are interesting to them and create solutions. The world does not want or need more people who are waiting to be told what to do.

The Maker Movement is not just *a* solution; it is ***the*** solution.

We are on the cusp of something great with this movement. If we were able to make just a few slight adjustments to school, creating learner-centered environments, it would transform the futures of millions and millions of kids.

Think about what it would do for the future of our nation; how it would change the landscape of company culture, and the level of happiness and joy in people's lives. Think of all the solutions that would be created to address life's toughest challenges. If we give kids REAL things to work on, talk to them, and spend more time asking them what they think, and then really listening to their responses...We will empower them to believe they are the creators of the future, and that the future can be bright for all people.

We can end poverty and apathy and give people something to really live for. We can drastically reduce the cycle of crime and punishment plaguing every corner of our society and we can create a world where empathy and respect and trust reign. Joyful education that engages hearts, minds and hands is the answer, and it will take all of us to bring this to life on the scale required to reach all kids.

> *"Making makes motivation!"*
> *Rick Fitzpatrick, Superintendent*

I'm not sure exactly what drew me to education nearly ten years ago, but I am glad it happened and I am exactly where I am supposed to be, empowering kids and teachers to take hold of the possibility that Maker education offers.

Equipment and Supply List

There are so many ways you can outfit a makerspace, so I want you to know this list is not the "end all be all" list of things you need or should have.

This is the list of things we used to make all of the activities listed in this book possible for the elective we created and we found it to be a good range of tools and supplies for the students.

This list is also available via a Google spreadsheet, with costs, links, extra notes and how many of each item we purchased. You can find that list here: http://bit.ly/29tDYjT

Technology

Wacom tablets
Adobe Creative Cloud software
iMacs
iPads
Covers for ipads
Charging cabinet

Freestyle Making and Building Supplies

Popsicle sticks
Rubber bands
White glue
Paperclips
String
Scissors
Measuring tape

Masking tape
Soldering kits
Copper tape
LED lights
Tools such as hammers, pliers, screwdrivers, etc.
Plastic cups
Markers
Ultimate cutter
Duct tape and washi tape
Keva Planks
LEGO Kits

Filming Area

Green screen
Mic
Mic mount (ringer)
Mic stand
Tripod (for steadying ipad for video) - the expense is due to getting a good tripod with a "fluid head" for quality movement.

Kits for Robotics and Coding

Arduino kits
Digital Sandbox (SparkFun - coding)
Lilypad design kit (wearable electronics)
Robotics - Parallax Arduino Shield
In hindsight, I would also include SparkFun's Makey Makey in this list

Other

Incidentals, batteries, etc for budgeting purposes
Glass wall for brainstorming and storyboarding (1/4" tempered glass)

Additional Resources

This is by no means an exhaustive list of all the great resources out there, but it will give you a really great list of places to go to learn more and cultivate connections beyond what we've given you here.

These are the websites and organizations that have been staples for me along the way. I've also enjoyed the support, inspiration and community I have developed on Twitter! I hope you enjoy!

Future Development Group, LLC:
www.futuredevelopmentgroup.com
@FutureDevGroup
Future Development Group offers in person and virtual support with Maker programs to places of learning all over the world. Our vision is that all students experience the joyful and relevant education they deserve and we are passionate about doing everything we can to make that happen. We regularly publish making and leadership related blog posts, maintain news about Maker events we are involved in and share Open Educational Resources (OER). Our blog is an ongoing mini version of what's in this book, so if you've enjoyed *180 Days of Making*, you can follow us and our work, through regular updates, conveniently delivered to your inbox.

Maker Education Initiative:
www.makered.org
@MakerEd
Maker Education Initiative (Maker Ed) is a nonprofit organization that envisions every young person having equitable access to engaging learning experiences that collectively develop their skills, knowledge, and ways of thinking, and that recognize and value their ability to experience and influence their world. To support educators and insti-

tutions in creating these kinds of engaging, inclusive and motivating learning experiences, Maker Ed provides training, resources, and community of support around maker education.

Maker education is a learner-driven, open-ended, interactive learning approach that can enable students of all ages, abilities, and backgrounds to develop new perspectives, a belief in their own abilities, and a passion for learning. Through our work, Maker Ed makes it possible for every educator in America -- with a particular focus on those in underserved communities -- to incorporate maker education into their learning environments in an easily accessible, highly-flexible way.

Maker Ed's online community on G+:
https://plus.google.com/u/0/communities/108516741770696736815

MAKE:
www.makezine.com
@Make
Makezine and Maker Faire are produced by Maker Media, a leader in the global maker movement. For more information about the magazine and to keep up on the world of making, visit Makezine.com. To find a Maker Faire near you or to participate in one of the events, visit MakerFaire.com. Maker Media also publishes a wide range of books on the tools and process of making.

Agency by Design
www.agencybydesign.org
@AgencybyDesign
Supported by the Abundance Foundation, Agency by Design (AbD) is a multiyear research initiative at Project Zero investigating the promises, practices, and pedagogies of maker-centered learning experiences.

Edutopia's Maker Section

www.edutopia.org

@Edutopia

A comprehensive website and online community that increases knowledge, sharing, and adoption of what works in K-12 education.

Project Ignite (from Autodesk)

projectignite.autodesk.com

@ProjectIgnite

Project Ignite enables learners of all ages to gain practical hands-on experience with new software and hardware to build literacy in design, 3D, electronics, programming and more.

SparkFun

www.sparkfun.com

@SparkFun

In addition to products, SparkFun offers classes and online tutorials designed to help educate individuals in the wonderful world of embedded electronics.

Thingiverse

www.thingiverse.com

@thingiverse

MakerBot's Thingiverse is a thriving design community for discovering, making, and sharing 3D printable things. As the world's largest 3D printing community, we believe that everyone should be encouraged to create and remix 3D things, no matter their technical expertise or previous experience. In the spirit of maintaining an open platform, all designs are encouraged to be licensed under a Creative Commons license, meaning that anyone can use or alter any design.

Tinkercad|

www.tinkercad.com

@tinkercad

Tinkercad is a simple, online 3D design and 3D printing tool for the masses. Whether you're a designer, hobbyist, teacher, or kid, you can use Tinkercad to make toys, prototypes, home decor, Minecraft models, jewelry – the list is truly endless!

Whoever you are... you dream it, you can make it - our goal is for you to become a proficient Tinkerer!

Instructables
www.instructables.com
@instructables

Instructables was officially spun out of Squid Labs in the summer of 2006, and has gone on to grow from a modest hundreds of projects to over one hundred thousand. The community that now calls the site home, is an amazing mix of wonder from around the world. Every day we continue to be amazed by the imagination, curiosity, and simple awesomeness of everyone who shares their creations with us on Instructables.

The Tinkering Studio at the Exploratorium
tinkering.exploratorium.edu
@TinkeringStudio

The Tinkering Studio promotes thinking with your hands while experimenting with art, science, technology, and delightful ideas. At the Exploratorium!

About the Author and Contributors

Michelle Carlson
Founder and CEO Future Development Group, LLC
Twitter: @FutureDevGroup

Author and consultant, Michelle Carlson, is an internationally recognized leader and change agent in education. She has been featured in various publications, was recognized with an American Graduate Champions award in 2015 and was nominated to be a White House Champion of Change for Making the following year.

She is a member of the American Indian Society of Scientists and Engineers, speaks regularly at conferences on the Maker Movement and serves in multiple leadership roles and as a board member of several education related nonprofits.

Michelle is, above all else, a social entrepreneur, believer in the power of "we" and lover of all things making. She is passionately devoted to building a better, brighter future for all, through her work, community service and network of like-minded dreamers and doers.

She is proud of the fact that she is a female entrepreneur, with a Bachelor's Degree in Information Technology. She will tell you, with a mischievous smile that she knows how to code, knit, sew, and rebuild classic cars and will follow that statement with, "and you can too!"

As CEO of Future Development Group, LLC, Michelle continues to build on her passion, providing places of learning with the support and resources they need to give all students the education they deserve. Her work has served as a catalyst in her community and region, inspiring a diverse group of leaders to come together collaboratively, think big and forge new pathways in unexpected places.

She lives with her hubby, dog, chickens and cats on a 10 acre tree covered paradise in the country and relishes the wide open sense of possibility that every day brings when she wakes up at 4 am.

Contributors:

Noelle McDaniel
Ed Tech Curriculum Support Provider and Teacher
Twitter: @NMcCammond21
Noelle (AKA teacher rock star!) has more than a decade of experience as a dynamic classroom teacher and was an integral part of the success of the program we've documented here.

She graciously provided many of the printable materials that are linked throughout the book, which made it even more of a gem for all those teachers out there looking for great ideas and inspiration.

Phil Mishoe
Teacher
Phil (also an amazing teacher rock star!) has been teaching middle school PE and coaching volleyball, basketball, and track for 18 years - all in Corning, Ca.

He was asked to teach a section of a brand new class called Adventures in Making for the 2015/2016 school year and, at the time, had very little knowledge of what Making was.

As you head into this grand adventure, Phil offers his advice, from a teacher's perspective:

"To say the least, I was very hesitant and nervous. That has all changed dramatically! What an eye opener it has been for me to be a part of such an innovative and exciting class.

There are so many possibilities with this style of class and teaching and to see the students get excited everyday and take ownership in their work was truly an amazing sight. It's extraordinary to watch what happens when you give your students the ability to figure something out for themselves and let them fail and watch how they fix their failures to turn them into successes."

The Prequel to the Story

In the epic style of one of my all-time favorite movie franchises, the story of how it all got started appears at the end. The following nostalgic reflection won't necessarily help you run your Maker elective class, but it was a critical piece of the puzzle for us in getting started here, and therefore an important part of the story that couldn't be left out.

In sharing the following reflections, and the story of how this happened, it is my hope that it offers you some insight into how we took on this monumental effort with little resources, so you can use that knowledge as power to create change in your own community. Being armed with the logistics of how others have done it is a huge start in making it happen in your own back yard.

Many times, when something really big happens, that big thing wouldn't have been possible without the things that served as a prequel to the story. The things that opened the road, making the bigger stuff possible. The Adventures in Making class is one of those big things.

Even before that, there was a chain of seemingly unrelated events that most definitely paved the way for the successes we had in Corning, CA. Some of those things paved the way for me to keep going. To keep pushing forward even when it was tough. Sometimes I wondered if I was trying to push a ten foot high cement wall, and other times it felt like I could lift that same wall, as if it were a feather, with just my words.

I came to be fully engrossed in this work several years ago when a friend came back from the Bay Area Maker Faire, excited about hosting a Faire in our rural Northern California county. As I heard her talking about how great it would be to do this, my first thoughts were, "Who will make things?" and "Where will they make them?"

At the time, we didn't have many teachers encouraging students to create as part of their learning, and even if a teacher wanted to do this, the tools, equipment and spaces to do so were nowhere to be found.

So we set out to create those missing pieces so that we could get started with the work of encouraging hands-on, minds-on learning as a way to approach education joyfully. Along the way, we encountered bumps in the road, some of which were bigger than others. We were given a space in the building where I worked to create a makerspace, which was wonderful, but there was little budget for furnishings or fixtures.

I had this grand dream of creating a space that reflected a kind of melding of urban design and steampunk flare. Something that would really wow people of all ages when they walked in. Something that would put them in a different mindset, just by *being there.*

> *I employed the concept fiction writers use to create "willing suspension of disbelief" in their readers, which, in essence, produces an experience allowing people to believe the unbelievable, and to suspend their normal logical faculties for the sake of enjoyment. I wanted everyone to feel a sense of overwhelming possibility and inspiration, just be being there. For a fantastic example of this concept, I highly recommend Mac Barnett's TED Talk "Why a Good Book is a Secret Door."*

As my co-worker and I researched the cost of tables and chairs with the kind of styling we were looking for, we realized right away that we were far out of our league. The tables we were looking at ranged in price from $1200 a piece to $2500 a piece and up. Yikes! We needed a new plan. We weren't willing to give up the dream of the amazingly inspiring space, but we definitely didn't have the money to make it happen in the usual way.

Enter a community supporter, my husband, the craftsman.

I came home from work one evening and told him about what I was trying to do and why. Knowing how important this was to me, and that it would be the catalyst for a whole new kind of learning for kids, he agreed to make everything I needed as a volunteer. I felt like jumping up and down and dancing right there. My dream would live, partly because I wouldn't give up until I found a way to make it happen.

The whole thing lived in my head, in full living color. I could see how beautiful the space would be and I knew intuitively the way it looked would matter a lot in how it made people feel, and how it opened kids' minds up to learning.

Even though I could see it clearly, and I knew I was onto something, it was difficult to get others to see it too. I wasn't expecting this piece to be so challenging, but it was. What they believed was more in tune with good curriculum creates good learning and the way the room looks really doesn't matter much. Argg!

Poverty Comes in Many Forms

Poverty has an entirely different meaning in places where diversity and opportunity are not plentiful - it's not just financial. It's poverty of ideas, poverty of inspiration, poverty of experience.

We were bringing very different ideas to an area that had long existed on a set understanding of "the way things are."

And then, I found Steve Davee via a web search one day while I was researching and learning about the Maker Movement and its role in education. Steve is the Chief Maker Educator with the Maker Education Initiative and a serious force for all that is good in this movement.

This is one of those little gems that helps us all remember that if you want something bad enough, you will keep knocking on doors until one of them finally opens. I sent him an email, out of the blue, hoping to connect and he agreed to a 15 minute Google Hangout. The conversation started out with him saying, "You know, I get a lot of requests and I have to be very careful about how I spend my time, so you have about 15 minutes here."

My brain started to race. Oh my gosh, 15 minutes? How will I make this work? Do I talk really fast, or do I re-prioritize what I was going to say, or something else? I turned my laptop around so he could see the room we were working on, and I gave him the virtual tour of the space while telling him what I intended to do once it was open. "We're going to have kids come via field trips and offer them an opportunity to learn about science and coding and electronics and art..." I went on and on in the best way I could to show him I was serious, I had a real plan and a truly grand vision.

At the end of my 15 minutes with Steve, he said, "I think we're going to need to talk again, and let's do an hour next time."

I remember the early days in all of this, not really having any idea what I was doing, or how I was going to do it. The only thing I knew for sure was that I needed to keep going. That I needed to bring my dream to life for kids. Steve was the very first person outside of my community to understand and encourage what I was trying to do and he was a huge part of what kept me going long enough to breathe life into my vision of what could be for our kids.

> *This story could be anyone's story. We have all been here and in sharing it with you, I hope to give you a glimpse into the real challenges we faced and how we made it happen anyway. Hard times happen. Don't let them stop you from reaching out, asking for help, and making it happen.*

Early on, we were invited to attend the Bay Area Maker Educator Meetups, an informal gathering of educators, passionate about experiential learning. The group meets every other month at San Francisco's famed Exploratorium. They were an amazing group of people and we learned a lot from them. It was a seven hour drive in all to get there and back, but worth every second. The biggest thing I got out of it was that we needed something like that up here. Not just for the professional development, but also for the community development. Our educators didn't have access to anything like that...until now.

All of a sudden we were connected with other people who "got it!" Now there was a bigger group of like-minded educators cheering us on. When our first makerspace opened in January of 2014 it was a huge hit!

> *Psst! Connections outside your own community are HUGE in making this work happen. The extra inspiration,*

encouragement and validation that comes from these kinds of experiences can make or break you when it comes to big work like this. Think MakerEd, Twitter, Google+, etc. Look for like-minded people who will help keep you simultaneously inspired and grounded and reach out to them!

Once our makerspace was open, teachers were bringing classes of students in for field trips and we were teaching things like coding, electricity, film making and art, with true joy. Instead of 30 kids struggling to stay awake, we had a sea of smiling faces, alive with curiosity and inspiration. AND they were still learning math and English and a host of other skills necessary for living a successful life.

We had a tangible example of what learning looked like when it was done in a way that truly had the best interest of the student at it's heart. Because kids were eating it up, so were the teachers, and the happy faces of the teachers got the attention of the administrators.

I started getting requests from school leaders all over the county to come and help them create similar learning environments in their schools and I quickly realized I had found that magical sweet spot in my career. Some people go their whole life searching for this, and never find it.

This is the thing Sir Ken Robinson calls The Element, which he states in his book, *The Element: How Finding Your Passion Changes Everything*, "is the point at which natural talent meets personal passion." He goes on to say that "when people arrive at the Element, they feel most themselves and most inspired and achieve at their highest levels."

I can tell you with 100% certainty that finding your Element is extremely powerful. And in finding mine, I knew beyond a doubt my purpose is to help kids find theirs. Creating these experiences and supporting others in making this kind of magic happen for kids and teachers has made me feel more alive than I've ever felt in my entire life.

So I did the only thing that made sense. I jumped. No, I dove; head first into the unknown, creating the company that would give me the freedom I needed to do this work on a larger scale. This leap was also what allowed us to create Adventures in Making.

> *It took more than just telling people we could make magic happen, it took rolling up our sleeves and showing them what it looked like in tangible ways, letting them experience it for themselves and then having the patience to wait for them to have their own light bulb moments, all so we could really begin the work. Remember this, because doing something tangible can sometimes make all the difference in the world in being supported.*

As a change agent in your own community, sometimes the most important thing you can do to make it happen, is to go first, and don't quit. Having faith that everyone else will catch up to you if you do your part.

Being an agent of change is a delicate dance and having people around you who fearlessly champion the work is an absolute necessity. I am so lucky to have those people with me here now, in my own community, as well as out there in the world. Without them, none of this would have ever been possible.

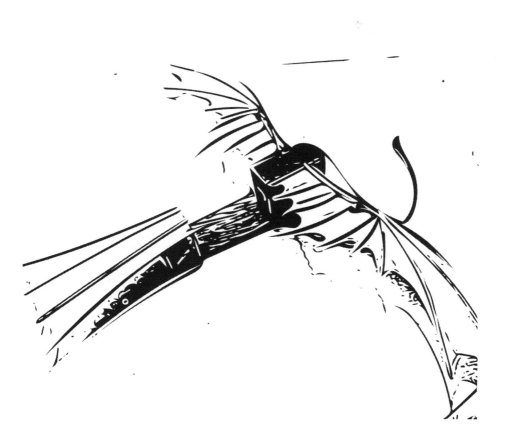

Special Thanks To...

I wish I could name all of the people I am grateful for in this work and in my life, but such a list would take up an entire book all by itself, and grows longer every day. I will have to make do with naming the following wonderful humans have who directly impacted the work that and made this book possible. I am deeply grateful to them all.

First and foremost, I must give credit to my parents, who taught me anything is possible, if you're willing to do the hard work to go after what you want. They raised me to be a brassy, caring, roll-up-your-sleeves, kinda girl who can find my way over, through or around any wall, fence, moat or other barriers I encounter. Now, because of what I learned from them, I get to pay it forward empowering kids in poverty, and in every kind of tough situation you can imagine. Thanks Mom and Dad!

Thanks to my very first mentor, Mary Jayne, who is one of the most savvy and wise business women I have ever met. Just about every day, I encounter some situation where your voice is strong in the back of my mind, helping me find my path, and stay the course.

Thanks to Maureen, who taught me how to be a great teacher and leader who tirelessly supports the work of amazing educators everywhere. In a lot of ways, you created the foundation I needed, allowing me to go far beyond where I started.

Thanks to Syerra who has been a dear-hearted inspiration to me in so many ways. Syerra is loved by all who know her and a true gift in my life. She taught me how to be a good manager and is probably the best and most loyal member of a team anyone could ever have.

Thanks to all of the superintendents and principals here in Tehama County, who encouraged me to take this giant leap of faith and do this work on a larger scale! Without you, I wouldn't have seen the wide open possibility that was in front of me. And, a special thanks to Rick, who directly supported this entire project. We have you to thank for making it all possible. You opened the road and kept it open.

Thanks to the entire team at Corning Elementary who supported us as we traveled the road and to those like Noelle and Phil, who graciously gave of their time to contribute to this book. You are heroes for kids!

Thanks to the very first Makerspacians! These four young people hold an incredibly special place in my heart. Even before I took the leap, your stories, struggles and triumphs moved me profoundly and fueled the work. It is for kids like you that I get up every day.

Thanks to Jonna, for your editing genius, your wisdom and guidance all these years, and for all the fun, laughter filled afternoon tea adventures!

Thanks to my dearest friend, my husband, Jim, who makes it possible for me to do this work; and with his own stories of school, has inspired me to tirelessly pursue more joyful education for all.

To everyone else, you know who you are, who support, encourage, fan flames, listen, tell stories, and do amazing work to make the world a better place for all of us, I thank you.

I owe a sincere debt of gratitude to the thousands of people who have had a hand in the journey.

Made in the USA
San Bernardino, CA
20 August 2016